Engaging Heaven for Trade

Living the Principles of a Traded Life

By

Dr. Ron M. Horner

Engaging Heaven for Trade

Living the Principles of a Traded Life

By

Dr. Ron M. Horner

LifeSpring International Ministries, Inc.
PO Box 5847
Pinehurst, North Carolina 28374
www.RonHorner.com

Engaging Heaven for Trade

Living the Principles of a Traded Life

Copyright © 2022 Dr. Ron M. Horner

Scripture is taken from the New King James Version®. Copyright © 1982 by Thomas Nelson. Used by permission. All rights reserved. (Unless otherwise noted.)

Scripture quotations marked (TPT) are from The Passion Translation®, Copyright © 2017, 2018 by BroadStreet Publishing Group, LLC. Used by permission. All rights reserved. ThePassionTranslation.com

Scripture marked (THE MIRROR) is taken from The Mirror Study Bible by Francois du Toit. Copyright © 2021 All Rights Reserved. Used by permission of The Author.

All rights reserved. This book is protected by the copyright laws of the United States of America. This book may not be copied or reprinted for commercial gain or profit. The use of short quotations or occasional page copying for personal, or group study is permitted and encouraged. Permission will be granted upon request.

Any trademarks mentioned or used are the property of their respective owners.

Requests for bulk sales discounts, editorial permissions, or other information should be addressed to:

LifeSpring Publishing
PO Box 5847
Pinehurst, North Carolina 28374
USA

Additional copies available at www.courtsofheaven.net

ISBN 13 TP: 978-1-953684-24-0
ISBN 13 eBook: 978-1-953684-25-7

Cover Design by Darian Horner Design (www.darianhorner.com)
Image: 123rf.com # 79154088

First Edition: November 2022

10 9 8 7 6 5 4 3 2 1

Printed in the United States of America

Table of Contents

Acknowledgements i
Characters Mentioned iii
Preface v
Chapter 1 Trading in Heaven 1
Chapter 2 Why Understand Trade Routes 13
Chapter 3 Truth in Trade 17
Chapter 4 Trade Routes 23
Chapter 5 The Golden Pathway 31
Chapter 6 Realms & Dimensions 39
Chapter 7 Paradigms 51
Chapter 8 Understanding Realms 57
Chapter 9 Trading Outside of Time 63
Chapter 10 Trading on Ungodly Bonds 75
Chapter 11 Understanding Trade Routes 83
Chapter 12 The Harvest of Trade 95
Chapter 13 The Hall of Commerce 103
Chapter 14 The Court of Trade 111
Chapter 15 Relationships & Trades 117
Chapter 16 Governing Our Realm for Trade ... 125

Chapter 17 Conclusion 133
Appendix 135
Learning to Live Spirit First 135
Description 143
About the Author 145
Other Books by Dr. Ron M. Horner 147

Acknowledgements

With much gratitude I want to recognize the outstanding work of my team who assisted me in the realms of Heaven and in the compilation of this book.

Anna Horan has also been helpful with editing this book. I honor them for their service to the King. Thank you.

Characters Mentioned

The following characters are mentioned in this book:

Abraham: an Old Testament patriarch.

Ezekiel: the chief angel over our ministry.

Francis: a woman in white who assisted us in the business complex.

Jackson: a man in white who instructs us from Heaven.

James: a man in white who assisted us in an engagement.

Lydia: a woman in white linen who advises our ministry.

Malcolm: a man in white who instructs us from Heaven.

Mitchell: a man in white who is one of our instructors.

Stephanie: my Executive Assistant.

Theodore: our heavenly professor's name.

Wisdom, Understanding, and Knowledge: three of the Seven Spirits of God.

——— · ———

Preface

Commerce for Sons & Daughters

In preparation for a podcast I was scheduled for, Lydia opened our engagement by reminding us that we needed to announce to our ministry audience that we were going to be guests on a podcast. We were told to make an announcement that we will soon have details to share regarding operating in the spirit and operating in heavenly realms for the purpose of business and trade. Heaven calls it "trade," while we call it "business." We agreed on the common denominator each term has of commerce. Lydia indicated that this would broaden the understanding of the sons and daughters of God in the Father's interest in every area of their life.

This topic of trade or business was what Lydia was talking about related to people who have a propensity or a desire to engage in commerce. (I tend to want to call it trade because that is what Heaven calls it.)

> *The essence of trade is that it is taking one thing and multiplying it.*

It is taking something, whatever we are trading—our commerce or our business idea—but it **must be done in righteousness.** It must be done in righteousness without the spirit of religion and in the freedom as a son of God, a son who has been given authority to create an expansion by the multiplication of his trade. When the sons and daughters of God begin to do this first from the spiritual realm or in conjunction with what Heaven has made available, economies will be impacted.

Heaven is making available some things, such as angels that are assigned to that individual and his enterprise, because there are things that we are never going to accomplish if we don't have the connection and the understanding of collaborating with angels in those things.

The circumstance of being in the world today **demands a deepening of our spirit man to stay linked to heavenly places for the expansion of longer, greater, expansive times in the realms of Heaven,** so that we become spatial people—people that interact in space AND time.

> *But since we are bringing this out of Heaven, we are the portal, the gate to this physical realm.*

The blessings of God are things like the knowledge of God, the blueprints of God, and all the plans that God has for the earth realm that are going to be constructed and built in the physical plane.

> *Yet, the reason they are going to be built and constructed in the physical plane is because righteousness is behind it. The righteousness of God is behind it.*

It is a spiritual activity to get that spiritual thought, blueprint, idea, knowledge, and/or understanding and to allow that to come through us.

> *We are the portal of God into the physical plane to see it made manifest in commerce and trade and how the righteousness of God is His perfection.*

It is the perfection of God that creates a set-apartness. (I do not want to use the word holiness because it sometimes carries baggage in people's minds.)

> *When the trade comes through a child of God and that child of God is trading on that righteousness and perfection, there is a grace on it.*

> *Even prophetically, what is coming down, what is coming to us in days ahead, is the ability to do this as sons and daughters of God.*

However, the first step of that is to realize we have access in Jesus to have our being in Heaven and to be taught, to learn, to gain knowledge and understanding, because this is what our inheritance is that God wants us to use on the earth right now. It is going to be different, and it is going to better.

It is going to be better in every facet and respect than what the world systems are doing—so much so that we, as sons and daughters of God, we are not even paying attention to what the world is doing. The world has simply become dim in our sight because our sight is so filled with what Heaven is releasing to us to do on the earth.

Focusing on Spiritual Realms First

It is the rub of determining to focus on spiritual realms first— "seek first the Kingdom of God,"[1] when the world is constantly shouting for our attention. Sons and daughters of God can learn the way of the physical things that will help them, like getting alone (whether it is early

---

[1] Matthew 6:33

morning or late afternoon), or whatever it takes for them to have the moment that they hunger and thirst after the Kingdom of God. Hunger and thirst after that, after the knowledge of Heaven. God wants to give us this knowledge. We must determine, "I'm going to go there. I am going to abide there. I am going to see there. I am going to hear there. I am going to understand there. I am going to connect there. I am going to turn my face there. I will concentrate on that so that I do not have to lack in anything, because I have this burning propensity and desire to release that much righteousness into a commerce, into a trade, into an assistance." That is the building of the Kingdom on earth as it is in Heaven.

Diametrically Opposed

There is much that the Father must teach about commerce and trade that are diametrically opposed to how the world has taught trade and commerce, because the spirit realm is the antithesis to the earth realm and the world systems. But this is God's great joke on the enemy, where the enemy thought he owned commerce, trade, the earth realm, along with world systems, and then the sons and daughters get involved in that arena.

Sometimes we must take a minute to let our imagination consider that the Father's heart is that the nations of humanity, the races of humanity, the reflections of His expression in all the people that are made in His image and likeness—that His desire is that they turn to those who are His sons and daughters. That they hunt them down to say, "I would rather trade with you. I would rather engage in commerce with you because when I do, it feels right. It increases me. It enlarges something more than just my physical living out on this planet. It connects me to something that is intangible that I cannot put my hand to, that I cannot put a name to."

Blueprints of Heaven

The blueprints of Heaven for business are full.

We could see a library and see blueprints hanging from racks. We saw rack after rack and room after room. There were blueprints for commerce and blueprints for trade. There were so many methods and manners of conducting business that we would not even have to copy someone else because we have our own blueprint. We have our own thing.

These are available to the sons of God, but the seeking after the Kingdom, the coming here (into Heaven), the ascension to the spiritual realm, the looking, seeing, hearing, waiting upon Heaven, the engagement with angels, the request to open portals of revelation—these things must be learned first.

First Things First

- Seeking after the Kingdom

- Ascension to the spiritual realm of Heaven
- Looking, seeing, hearing, and waiting upon Heaven
- Engaging with angels, and men and women in white linen
- Requesting Heaven to open portals of revelation

Then, as these things are learned, as we get good at them, the next step of that journey would be, "Okay, what is in Heaven for me that I need, so that I can do what You have called me to do?"[2]

We haven't even talked about how to accomplish this out of time. We are just talking about how to bring it out of time and into the time realm.[3] We have not even talked about how to conduct commerce and trade in spiritual realms. Part of that is because it is tied to an era and a time and season.

We want to release a blessing of grace to those individuals who want to engage in commerce and trade. We want to release the grace of Heaven, the grace that is Heaven, the grace of Heaven that is available for us to do a trade in the earth realm as we operate from Heaven down™.

---

[2] My book *Living Spirit Forward* talks about these concepts in more depth. It will help you greatly as you learn to build your life and business from Heaven downward.

[3] The spirit realm is outside of time, so bringing something heavenly to the earth realm is from out of time into time.

Chapter 1

Trading in Heaven

As with other books I have written, they are the result of engagements with Heaven—often with my Executive Assistants, but not always. Some were borne of personal journaling times or other personal encounters. I had been waiting to learn about this subject for a long time and was asked by someone while standing at the Help Desk in the Business Complex in Heaven if we would like a lesson on Heaven's commerce and trade.[4] Of course, we were open to anything that Heaven wanted to share with us.

A man walked into the room carrying an encyclopedia. He immediately began to teach us concerning trade, which is the exchange of goods and services.

---

[4] This chapter is from *Building Your Business from Heaven Down* but is included in this book as it gives a good understanding of trading floors and trading from Heaven's perspective.

> *Trade from Heaven's realm is galactic.*

It spreads through all universes, all timelines, and all dimensions. It is accessed by faith in Jesus Christ, the Son of God.

We can engage in this trade on many levels. Our spirit is active in trade during the night seasons when our soul and flesh are asleep. A believer's spirit, having awakened to Holy Spirit, and in conjunction with the indwelling Holy Spirit, is made alive unto God. That person's spirit then begins to go on assignments for the Kingdom of God. Sometimes Holy Spirit comes to us in our dreams, and we can watch the trades in the dream. These dreams are the type that are often easily forgotten or last for just a moment upon awakening. Our spirit is the part of us that trades in heavenly realms.

We can step into our spirit and accomplish visits any time, the way we have been learning to do. Many of the saints have been unaware of this or if they have known of it, they call it by names other than trade. Sometimes they refer to it as the prophetic, which is not the most accurate way to view this.

Sometimes the trade from the spirit realm is a prophetic word, bringing a trade of Heaven into the earthly realm. The saints of God are assigned to this and associated with this work. This is the work of hands and deeds.

However, the working out of trade routes, trading floors, and the activity of trade from Heaven is like this: if we begin in Heaven first, we are always going to see it manifest in the earth realm secondarily. We have not been aware that this was what was manifesting—that we made a trade in Heaven.

Our spirit made this trade on behalf of our soul and flesh, especially if we are awakened soldiers of the Lord. In Scripture, this is often referred to as armies of God, and the saints are operating as the armies of God (or in this capacity). Looking at it instead as being Ambassadors of the Kingdom of God is a keener, more focused way to see it or view it.

It was explained to us that indeed there are warlike things that must be done through the spirit realm.

Trade from Heaven is the work of the sons of God under the ambassadorial status that they hold in the earth realm

---

This has begun to change the earth and will completely transform it.

Functions of Holy Spirit

We were informed that the trading floors of Heaven are associated with the functions of Holy Spirit, the work in the spirit realm, and the conducting of courtroom work, which is essential to the trades at some level. Even a nominal trade in the earth realm has a counterpart in the Courts of Heaven. We would not be able to make a trade in the earth realm if the realm of the Courts of Heaven were not active on our behalf. The way they are intertwined cannot be underestimated or understated.

There has been grace from the Father on this for a long while, solely because the Bride has been blinded, veiled, and unable to hear. However, as the Bride's senses are awakening and she gains an understanding of who she really is and the work of the season in which she is alive on earth, this change in paradigm is gaining momentum exponentially.

Remember the season called the "Word of Faith" movement? Even this was an attempt to engage trading floors of Heaven, although in an immature way.

> *The Father will not allow us to stay immature for long, as His desire is to grow His children up in every way.*

Thus, one season ends, and new seasons come.

When the Bride experiences these nuances of change as the Father releases into the earth, she develops a better understanding of what the work is that she is here to do. This can be seen through what we call the movements of the church in the earth age.

The trading floors of Heaven exist to expand the Kingdom of God, not only in the earth realm but in the unseen galactic areas as well.

This is little known, but pioneers and forerunners are beginning to launch into it. For our purposes, a more grounded experience in the realms of Heaven that pertain to commerce is needed. This book will be a good place for beginners to begin with and concentrate on.

We ascertained that the galactic areas of trade will be revealed in a future season. As further revelation is revealed to the saints who operate in the realms of Heaven, they will be the first to become aware and sense an opening of that door. However, that is a very narrow way right now.

The Majority Need

For us to remain in our course right now and to operate from the majority need would be the Father's preference. What is most needed right now is to understand that the realms of Heaven can be accessed for what we on earth call natural commerce, natural trade, and natural business. Such a great need exists for the Bride to begin to access this inheritance given to her. It is currently barely accomplished.

We have seen the Bride attempt this many times, but she often enters with demands like a small child as opposed to considering how Heaven could help her. She often comes with her own list of wants and needs, which is not what Heaven has in mind—just like a parent would not agree that candy makes an ideal meal.

A grace and mercy exist for this, as Heaven knows the Bride is simply growing up. What we have learned about the Business Complex of Heaven seems fantastical to many. It may even seem unrelated to them. They are going to have a challenging time connecting it to their reality. Thus, we must continue to remind the believers that this is a faith activity. Furthermore, it is also an activity of worship and is divinely written—we would call this the 'activity of the saints' which is written upon scrolls and books.

The Kingdom of God, because it is based on a system of government, sometimes trips up members of the Bride because they are unsure how business and government work together. They don't see the relationship between the two, and they miss the fact that the Bride has access to the Courts of Heaven through which all government and business should function.

All government and business should function through the Courts of Heaven.

Thus, it is not simply a place where the Bride brings her list of wants and needs, but a place of sitting down together to gain knowledge and strategy, to comprehend from the courts what the resistances are that need to be worked out. Furthermore, verdicts must first be attained from the Courts of Heaven, so the capabilities of the realm of business and trade are made easier in the earth realm.

Humanity has done this backwards for a long time and has slowed the pace of maturing by not recognizing the spirit realm and its desire to help and assist in these ways. But that is changing!

Even now, the Bride and its members are meant to be the shining example of this manner of existence on earth. This will allow unbelievers to come to know the awe of the access that we have to Heaven and to know that they do not have this access. This will cause them to desire the kingdom and will open the door to the work of Holy Spirit, first for salvation and then for working out of all parts of redemption in their own activity, the activity of their family, and within their own bloodlines.

The Centrality of Heaven

What cannot be underestimated is the significant role of the heavenly realm to one's daily activity in business and commerce on the earth. Some have known this through legal means because of the working out of their own attempts at power and profaning worship.

It is sad, but sometimes the Bride must learn from what the enemy is playing out. This will allow them to see what they do not have because they have not been aware of their ability to access what they have in Heaven.

It is time for the Bride to understand that she no longer needs to be blind to this. This blindness has been an outworking from the realm of darkness; its time is short, but it has had a field day plundering from the Bride the spiritual resources that are reserved for her. All of Heaven recognizes a pivotal change must occur, including the illumination of the Bride so that she can take her rightful place in operating from these realms. The resources of Heaven are plentiful and readily available, but little accessed.

It is unfortunate that those who are accessing these resources from spiritual realms access it through illegal means and are plundering what was intended for the Bride.

Heaven has a great interest in seeing a basic book, such as the one we are writing, to be disseminated among the Bride for her consideration, for it will take some time to process before even the minds of these believers are able to access by faith the information being written.

Heaven noted that this will confront the believer's understanding. It will cause some to hunger. Some will be motivated because they realize what they have been missing, and their anger at having been befuddled by the enemy will begin to play out for their good. Some will simply be unable to receive, having been captured by demonic plots and the outworking of injustice within their bloodlines.

Plainly put, some will have to continue in their ignorance until they step on Heaven's side of the veil forever, whereupon they will be welcomed to know what we now know. At that point, they will receive the unction that was available in the earth realm, but they either refused to agree with or were trapped by their unawareness as it played out against their life.

The Father does not have a judgment against these individuals, but He looks forward to the day when they operate from the heavenly side of the veil to help the Bride. Many are reserved for that, even as they are in their ignorance in the earth, so we do not have anything against them. We simply wait out their scroll of destiny and their time of stepping into Heaven.

Access is Free

Many believers look for this realm of Heaven, without knowing that their spirits can access it freely. They long for it from their souls. They do not understand that the operation of the soul will never access the realms of Heaven on its own. Many have been caught up in religiosity and its futile attempts to break down barriers that can only be broken down by the indwelling power of Holy Spirit as it awakens the Bride's individual members.

Some saints have seen the resources of Heaven. A few have even seen warehouses in the realms of Heaven that contain fantastical things, such as ones that are accessible for healing where body parts are available, or places containing blueprints of innumerable objects. The challenge is to keep pressing in for these things. We have been much thwarted in this even though we may not realize the level of resistance against which we are working. At the same time, the number of angelic assignments to help us gain this access in the earth realm is at work, too.

Many have ascertained parts of this through the pressing in of worship. Some also press in through fasting, or in whatever way they think of as "pressing in" to gain more access. However, the Father's heart is to help these individuals understand the simplicity of stepping into the realms of Heaven through Jesus, the Son. In this realm, because we are acting by faith when we access the realms of Heaven, our spirits are gaining strength and endurance to do this more.

Even as we have understood the paradigm between what the flesh goes through when we spend time, extended time, like this in heavenly realms—we will notice the strength that our soul, spirit, and flesh gain; eventually it plays out differently. We gain the strength and endurance to stay in heavenly realms longer and with less effect on the flesh each time. Heaven has help waiting for us there each time we come.

The ability to trade first from Heaven and then in the earth realm is extensive and more than we could think or know, greater than we could hope or imagine.

It is okay to imagine large and hope for big, but the mature saint comes into the realms of Heaven to know what is available to them that day so they may access it.

The immature saint comes in either with a laundry list of needs or without understanding the vast resources of Heaven which they could access. Some even come in still wearing the vestige of fear. This fear stems mostly from their soul, while their spirit is hungry to engage this realm. It is that vestment of fear which their soul wears that makes their time here difficult and laborious.

The grace the Father gives is this:

> *The longer a person spends pressing in or seeking after the Kingdom, the less challenging or laborious it is each time.*

The Father's will is for the Bride to encourage one another in these things, helping those who are still young and immature, as we are doing, and stirring up their faith by the testimony of what we have received.

This goes further than we think in helping those who are blinded because of existing covenants with darkness within their bloodline or simply because they do not know and are ignorant, not having been taught. Stir up one another's faith with the testimonies of the realms of Heaven. This is a spiritual trade, which in turn brings glory to the Father.

The instruction was clear. We must begin to think in new paradigms of trade. This is a great leap of faith, but it is the type of leap that brings impressive results. We must also start training our minds to think in terms of trade, for this is how the realms of Heaven operate. Think in terms of the government of the heavenly realm and its effect in all other realms, with the movement of resources from the heavenly realm to the earth realm by faith. The language of trade is a new language to learn in this decade.

> *The resistance to operating from the realms of Heaven will always stem from the natural realm.*

The resistance to operating from the realms of Heaven will always stem from the natural realm, but as we learn to eat more from the fruit of the Tree of the Knowledge of Life that is in the heavenly realm, the less we will hunger after the Tree of the Knowledge of Good and Evil. As that hunger craving changes, it will translate to spending more time receiving from Heaven in realms of Heaven. It is this way even now and always has been.

Chapter 2
Why Understand Trade Routes

Adam was given an instruction to tend the garden early in his existence. This was his initial trade in the realm of earth. He was given instruction to tend it, keep it, and subdue it—to bring it under his dominion. That requires diligence on the part of the groundskeeper to keep the tendencies of the earth in check.

This trade was initiated by the Father on behalf of His son. I remember hearing James Robison (the evangelist) share years ago how he was complaining to the Lord about the weeds in the garden he was tending at his home. He asked the Lord, "Why are there weeds?" The Lord promptly replied, "To teach discipline to the gardener." That is where we are today. We must learn the disciplines of trading from Heaven and with Heaven.

The Father has built into plants to produce. They do not have to be convinced to do that. They will do so automatically. However, if we learn the principles of growth for that plant, we can maximize the yield coming forth from it. It is a matter of stewardship. As we steward what is in our hands, it will grow. It is designed to.

The purpose of trade is for power, but what is done with that power is the real issue.

Most of us have never been taught of the concept of trade and trade routes in Heaven. Therefore, the benefit of these truths will pass us by because we are not engaging a principle of honor, which is:

What we honor we will have the benefit of.

It is difficult to honor what we have no understanding of. Therefore, Heaven has graced me and my team with several engagements with Heaven related to trade and trade routes.

In one of our earliest forays into the realms of Heaven, we were surprised to find Heaven wanting us to gain understandings on these matters.

A vision of ships in the heavens coming from multiple places in the cosmos toward earth could be seen. Not understanding all that Heaven was saying, we asked to be taught. We have not understood that other beings from distant places want to trade with us. They have information, technology, and more that they are willing to share with us, but we must open the door of access to the information. I realize this sounds like something from the Men in Black movie franchise, but they got the idea from somewhere.

Movies have been made about these things and have been presented in a humorous light, but they still contain understandings that we can glean from regarding trading in the heavenlies. Are we willing to be taught?

The information in these chapters provides things to consider, but moreover, it provides shortcuts to even deeper revelation that the Body of Christ needs currently.

In Genesis 11:26, we read the first mention of Abram (later called Abraham). Abraham is important in that he traded with Heaven and became extremely wealthy—so much so that his brother Haran's son, Lot, became jealous of Abraham's wealth and sought to duplicate Abraham's success. Of course, he had not learned how to trade with Heaven effectively and ended up in Sodom. At one point in Abraham's life, he was face to face with the King of Sodom when Abraham made a bold statement to the wicked king:

> *I have raised my hand to the LORD, God Most High, the Possessor of Heaven and Earth;* [23] *that I will take nothing, from a thread to a sandal strap, and that I will not take anything that is yours, lest you should say, 'I have made Abram rich.'* (Genesis 14:22-23)

His statement included a declaration of who he viewed as his provider—the LORD, God Most High, the Possessor (Creator) of Heaven and Earth. He understood that Heaven, Earth, and all their resources were owned by the Lord of Hosts not by any earthly king. He understood stewardship, which is a vital understanding concerning trading with Heaven. Abraham had gone with his father to the land of Canaan, and by cooperating with God, became a wealthy man who was well-respected among the nations of that time.

His life can provide clues and patterns that can be heeded as we learn about trading with Heaven. Remember, this is a man who was willing to trade his own son to please the Lord! The Lord himself replicated a similar scenario according to John 3:16.

———·———

Chapter 3

Truth in Trade

The subject of this engagement with Heaven was "The Subversion of Truth." Subversion is "the undermining of the power and authority of an established system or institution."[5]

Everyone believes they have a version of truth. People grow up believing *their* version of the truth—that it *is* truth, but that is just the thing: it is *their* version of the truth. Seeking the truth from the Father is a whole separate means of knowing truth of living, truth of becoming. The deception is *believing our own version* of truth. The truth of truth is the most impactful thing in a person's life. The despairing of truth in people's lives comes from their own lack of understanding that they are walking in a truth that is not their own. It has come down from the family line. *That* is their version of truth. That is where the rubber meets the road.

---

[5] Yahoo.com/Search=subversion+definition

People must seek the Father's truth for them. They must lay aside what is *believed* to be true and ask the Father. He is willing—He is wanting to lay all true truths before His sons, even the smallest measure. Wisdom is standing *BY* truth, Understanding and Knowledge all are there for the sake *of* truth. This is a lesson for all. This is a point of laying down ourselves. It means laying down everything at the cross, to the feet of Jesus and asking Him the question, the one who will give us the truth. Ask, seek, and knock, and we will find this truth.

We all have a version of truth that we believe in ourselves—truth about family, truth about our lives and it could be just that: our own version. We need to put everything down to Jesus and say to Him, "I believe this about myself. Is it true? Or is it not?" He will give that person who asks for the absolute truth, no matter big or small, the truth. Even the smallest truths, if they have a bit of untruth in them, it makes the whole matter untrue.

The only way to walk in this life is with 100% knowledge of who we are *in* truth. This is about us laying everything before the Lord—old mindsets and religious thinking. This will allow people to ask this of themselves, and especially regarding religious thinking, and it is imperative.

Halls of Trade

If we think about it, people don't realize that in everything they do, they are trading in and out of Heaven *or* in and out of hell. It is a choice, but sometimes, not having proper truths can cause them to trade out of the wrong destiny and out of the wrong place. They don't even realize that they are doing it. It is a sneaky way the enemy has intercepted their lives, which is why TRUTH is necessary to know, so that they can know where they are trading from and who are they trading to. Which place do they want to trade from?

We need to look at the reality that every word we say and everything that we do is a trade. It's a choice which creates.

The deception is *that even minor trades with hell won't really affect a person's life*—that *it won't really go anywhere over a person's life* when in fact, **hell will take that evil trade, that simple trade, and they will trade it and cause a "trade upon trade."** It will really get a person in a jam.

People get caught up in works. They want to *work* on behalf of the Kingdom and *work* their way through the Kingdom which comes from religious thinking. Everything is a choice. If they choose to love their neighbor, or if they choose not to, that's a trade. If they choose to come into agreement with a sin or a disease, that's also a trade.

The reason the Father calls us to walk the walk that He calls us to walk in *is because* Godly trades are made when we do that.

There is a means to keep people off the Godly path, where the enemy can trade the simplest thing and create a horrible path—a path filled with traps.

Simple words and simple acts of agreement with Heaven can create a major trickle-down effect of good upon a person's life. This trickle-down effect of small things snowballing into bigger things works the exact same way in the kingdom of darkness.

Men and women in white are taking these simple trades of good, and they are causing and creating a greater trade upon that person's life— like dividends.

It is the rule of multiplication. At the Father's hand, everything is multiplied for our good. That is Heaven's best. That's how He turns what was meant for evil into good. It is done from this place.

We don't have to understand it all right now, but the initial understanding is that the Father multiplies these good trades *on our behalf*. That is what is important. That's why making choices of truth, accepting His truth, desiring His truth, seeking out His truth, and walking in His truth are so important.

The Father multiplies our Godly trades. The enemy steals and divides. He trades upon those to create further darkness upon our lives.

Seek first the Kingdom of God and all of its righteousness and all of these things will be added unto you. (Matthew 6:33)

Chapter 4

Trade Routes

This engagement was quite different from others we had experienced. It began with a vision of the planet Earth, with what looked like beams of light intersecting or going from outside into the earth realm. No pattern could be detected, although the light was amber in color. These denoted the trading routes which are being traded on in the earth realm.

The vision shifted slightly, and it was as though we were in a ship traveling these trade routes. We were high above, looking down at the Earth, which was about the size of a basketball. We were travelling back and forth, going through the planet. These vessels came from all directions. Some looked as though they went straight through the planet to the other side, and some appeared to land on the Earth's surface. These were shipping lanes. They made the earth look like a porcupine with all the lights projecting from it, and they seemed sturdy.

These lanes were made of light beams, but they looked solid. Ships could be seen moving on them. We could see a ship come in, pass through the earth, and go to the other side. When they arrived at the earth realm, there was a certain place where they were off-loaded and their supplies distributed throughout the earth realm. It looked like it was being done from the interior of the earth outward toward the crust.

Once the ships come in and are unloaded, the materials on them manifest in the natural but are from other realms. They have value, but they are hard to describe because they come from a greater dimension into ours. The things we saw were the ancient pathways of trade. They have been established for a long time.

Some of the gates or harbors we refer to are ones that harbormasters control the access through. They could let the ships come in and out for much of Earth's history. Some in humanity have been aware of this, but the population is not aware.

A book was handed to us to read from, which spoke of the Old Testament patriarch Abraham:

> *In ancient times, the paths of trade from realm to realm were well known. Abraham operated in this. He did not always know about this, but once he came into an understanding of it, he became very wealthy in the earth. This was the plan of God for him. Multiplication became a well-known part of worship of the one true God, and wealth was accumulated, although it had to be sanctified.*

That sanctification took place with Melchizedek in his exchange with Abraham. From that point on, trade in the earth was allowed.

Abraham's household began to accumulate knowledge and understanding of this method of trade in and out of the shipping lanes of the earth. This knowledge had something to do with the trouble between Lot and Abraham. Lot had seen Abraham function in this and studied how he did it. He determined to launch out on his own and left Abraham, although it did not go well for him.

At this point in our engagement in Heaven, the professor (who had come in earlier but remained silent) began to teach us. What we saw were ancient trading lanes.

He began to teach us on this subject, and we began to understand that...

> The church is meant to be
> the gatekeepers and allow or disallow
> what goes in and out
> on the trading lanes.

This takes surrendering to spiritual things because it is highly contested by forces of darkness. Believers must do this through Jesus, from His realm. He has authority in all realms. His word is the final word, but often human populations trade through dark pathways or allow ungodly trades. In their ignorance, they become the recipient of these trades.

When humans are operating outside of the mind of Christ, the knowledge of the seven spirits of God, and the work of Holy Spirit, they are easily deceived. This deception can happen quickly and sometimes violently to the point that they become blind to what has become of their trade and the fact that they are being used.

This is illustrated in the story of Pharaoh and the children of Abraham in Egypt. Nevertheless, God will always raise up one to operate as a Redeemer, and in Christ, each can operate to redeem the pathways of trade. Some are called to this while others are not.

The trades that are coming and going from the earth on these ancient pathways are not really intended for humanity to prosper with, although humanity will still multiply, because it is right that the workers would gain part of the trade. Because the harbormaster is paid for his work of allowing or disallowing what comes through his port, he prospers.

What has happened is that the people who have lost sight of the proper reason for trade have illegally launched themselves into garnishing the trade itself. They have fallen into darkness and descended into what the Bible calls the lust of money. It does not go well with them. Nevertheless, they may still get wealthy off it. This has gone on for a long time and continues to the present day.

It falls to the sons of God to learn how to bring cases to the courts that will bring verdicts that lead to illegal trading being shut down. It will also allow the armies of Heaven to operate on these verdicts against the illegal operators of these trades. Very few court cases along these lines have been brought to the Righteous Judge. However, it is happening more now than ever before. This is not about prayer and intercession. This is about court cases and verdicts. This is about increasing the courtroom work of the Body, the Bride of Christ. This is about taking up the birthright and inheritance of their true calling, to see to it that the illegal operations, the garnishing of trade routes, and the stealing, theft, illegal access, or deportation of things are stopped.

---

*Heaven intends for soul parts
and even new natural body parts
to manifest in the earth realm.*

Those are being traded on in some of these shipping lanes. When they are offloaded from the ships, they get waylaid because of the wicked.

---

*Remember, a harbormaster
is a gatekeeper.*

Wanting to know where the resources from all these other realms come from, we were given understanding that if we look at the twelve tribes of Israel and what they traded from, each excelled in different areas. These things became their trade to one to another, so the whole universe (or rather, the multi-verse, which is all the realms collectively) prospered.

The church on planet Earth is part of a vast trading network of things that are meant to prosper all the realms.

The church has been given all things created by Elohim with all things being provisioned by Him. The earth realm is unique in that the glory of God is contained in humanity and in the person of Jesus.

There is an interconnection of trades, time and seasons, and the trade of items.

The realms all fit together in a matrix that is meant to operate well when it is operating according to how Elohim created it. However, it is still being contested because the devil has not yet been thrown down in finality. While the thief has lost ground, he is still in operation.

Legal Operators

Malcolm, who had joined us, explained that the gatekeeper (aka the harbormaster), and the church as the redeemed, are to be the legal operators of these trade routes in the earth realm. If every person on the planet were redeemed, then everyone would be able to operate this way. This is not the case, but we do have a remnant of redeemed ones who are coming into the understanding of this.

> *The redeemed sons of God occupy an eminent position in the earth, which they are coming to understand.*

They are learning the importance of their words and speech.

> *For centuries, the distraction has been to speak what we see in the natural rather than speaking by faith as an awakened spirit.*

Satan is upset that we are learning about this. He has had unrestrained use of the realms of darkness in trade for millennia, and no one had an inkling that he could or ought to be stopped, nor how to do that. But that will be changing.

This is all part of the greater works that Jesus spoke about when He told the disciples He had many things to tell them, but He could not tell them right then for they would not be able to bear it. Visualize a bear who is lurking to steal from everyone who comes into understanding. If anyone comes near to this revelation on trade and trade routes, the bear is ready to launch out and steal this. Often, this bear will bring fear, which makes humanity feel like grasshoppers in the sight of giants. All of that which they talked about in Scripture concerning understanding trade was because of this bear, whose job in the supernatural is to either make one afraid of this revelation or make one feel so small that they do not believe they have any chance of success.

Chapter 5

The Golden Pathway

As we engaged Heaven this day, Lydia took Stephanie and me on an alternate path than the one we typically used. We came through the Halls of Commerce. Along the way, Malcolm joined us, and we continued walking. We sat on the back row of the Court of Trades.

Stephanie described what she was seeing by saying, "Right now, I see the Just Judge doing paperwork. I see Jesus with His crown on, and I see men and women in white. I see what looks like princes and several accusers of evil over to the right." She paused to ask for counsel from the court and then continued, "The ones over to my right—some are princes, the others are accusers. They are present to disrupt the trades that are brought forward, but they are seated in the back. They are not up front like they are about to do something."

Speaking to Malcolm, Stephanie asked, "Can you tell me more about why we're here?"

"Yes," Malcolm replied.

Stephanie acknowledged, "We did want to know about trading routes."

"Do you see the council in this room?" he inquired.

Stephanie observed, "I see Jesus as the main counsellor. I see stadium seating. To the left of that are men and women in white, but they have a higher authority than we typically sense."

The counsel stated, "They are witnesses."

We asked, "Malcolm, are you letting us know that the cloud of witnesses bear witness to our trades?"

In response, Malcolm had us watch the court. Stephanie said, "I'm seeing this play out where an individual is trying to have a trade with Heaven, and the enemy comes to disrupt that with judicial paperwork. However, the cloud of witnesses is present on behalf of that person (the defendant) and are speaking for his generations."

She observed, "I've never quite seen it like that before, Malcolm. We know that the enemy comes to talk bad about our generations and keep us in bondage because of our generations, but you are saying that the cloud of witnesses speaks on behalf of the generations, too."

As we got up to leave Stephanie asked Malcolm, "Can you tell me about the spiritual matter regarding what we just saw?"

Malcolm said, "It matters because many times the accuser can bring legal paperwork *against* the generational line, but there is also legal paperwork *for* the generational line."

In reply Stephanie said, "Malcolm, I have never thought about it like that. I've continued to think about my generational line as being so wicked, and they were in many ways. But that is not the whole story."

Malcolm reminded Stephanie of her grandmother, who was a wonderful woman. Stephanie said, "She didn't seek out wickedness. It was just in her bloodline."

Malcolm said, "There are those that testified on her behalf."

We left the courtroom and went down a hallway to what looked like the Strategy Room. As we entered, we could see maps everywhere. Stephanie said to Malcolm, "Tell me about these maps that we see everywhere."

Malcolm replied, "These are the locations in time and out of time, in different dimensions, in a generational line where trade routes have been disrupted."

Stephanie said, "I am seeing it like coordinates."

Malcolm continued, "The maps also show where there have been good trades—Godly trades made in a person's generation.

Many times, the Godly trades outweigh the iniquities.

You have been hyper-focused on the iniquity in the bloodlines and Heaven wants you to see the Godly trades as well."

Stephanie replied, "Well, Malcolm, I guess I have been viewing my whole family line as completely corrupt, but there is much good in them, too. I see that now. Thank you."

How is this established?

We then sat down at a little table in the room. We began to see what looked like a matrix that Malcolm wanted to discuss. The matrix looked like what a net would look like on top of something. It was a grid. The Father put this matrix up before He even created the earth. The lines of the matrix are like pathways. They are like choices.

We could envision at this point when someone was with the Father in the beginning, prior to creation, where we were like a child, but it was really our spirit. We were not really a child, but we were innocent. We saw the innocence of this person before any corruption. They were having a conversation with the Father, and He was lovingly telling them about their path upon the earth. The person then stood and when they did, the grid came from up above the table to lying flat on the table. On the grid was a starting point to a path. It was like a Golden Pathway (a timeline) that the Father wanted them to walk, but there are these other side routes too. They are like choices we can make that get us off that timeline.

Every time we make a choice, it has been a trade. To visualize this image: We are on a Golden Pathway with a square to our left, one to our right, one is above us, and one below us. As we are walking this pathway, we get diverted and go through one of the many squares just described that we saw.

> *It is not the will of the Father for us to be sidetracked, because he does not want us to be hurt.*

He does not want us to experience all those things.

When we get off the Golden Pathway, and as we go through that square that is off our path, it is as if we are paying a toll to demonic entities when we decide to take that path. There are many ways back to the Golden Pathway, but there is an ungodly trade that has already been made. The minute that wrong decision is made in the spirit, it is an agreement and a trade. It is meant to set us up on a terrible path of destruction and iniquity, etc. But the one path that we see from the Father is so brilliantly lit up. There are opportunities upon this grid that are not on this straight path, opportunities where there are places to make good trades that lead us back to that straight, Golden Path. We will find opportunities in places to trade for good, even as there are just as many places to trade into evil.

If people can understand like they understand the concept of money—paying a dollar for a goods or service—it is the same concept in the spirit. They are paying a toll, and they are giving a piece of themselves. It is like they are taking a piece out of themselves (which can include DNA), and they are handing it over to the enemy as a trade.

> *The Father has provided many ways to get those that have traded out of themselves back to themselves.*

One of the main reasons for the Consequential Liens revelation was to redeem trades from the generations. Also, the angels seek to capture all that was lost, along with the innocence that gets restored using the Pink Capture Bag revelation. We were created in Innocence. Envision a person back at the very beginning in Innocence, standing before the Father. It is not just a person standing before the person. It is also Innocence standing before the Father.[6]

If all were able to hear and see this process of taking a piece of us and trading it, if we could understand that concept (and we will)—then there is a greater chance of making a better decision in the moment where we are tempted, and with that reality before us, not to take the other path.

---

[6] See the segment on the Pink Capture Bags in the book *Dealing with Trusts, and Consequential Liens in the Courts of Heaven*, LifeSpring Publishing (2022).

> *This grid always leads us back to the path we agreed to with the Father.*

This is the path where He said to us, as Innocence, "This is the path I want you to walk. On this path, all the Kingdom of Heaven is available for you."

> *When we step off that Golden Pathway, the iniquities of the generations cause trading into the kingdom of darkness.*

At different points on this grid where somebody may have traded into darkness, we can also see multiple trades into righteousness, and the cloud of witnesses are present at that place.

> *An individual witness is present at each point where that person has decided to trade with the Father.*

It is as if that cloud of witnesses continually turns us back towards the Golden Path again. That's why our steps matter.

When a person takes that step and trades into darkness, it is as if, in that moment, like when we go to a circus and we pay the person at the ticket booth—in this case, when the person makes the trade, hordes of demons come towards that person and begin walking in step with them. That is what we get back in return when we make that sort of trade.

The steps of the God-pursuing ones follow firmly in the footsteps of the Lord, and God delights in every step they take to follow Him. [24] If they stumble badly, they will still survive, for the Lord lifts them up with His hands. (Psalms 37:23-24)

Chapter 6
Realms & Dimensions

A question had arisen about something that had been briefly mentioned in a prior engagement, where we had been taught by Heaven about there being twelve heavens and thirty-three dimensions. For clarity, I asked if realms were within dimensions. Mitchell's instruction is summarized in this chapter.

We can think of the twelve heavens as vertical, from earth up. The thirty-three dimensions are classifications of other containers that hold varieties of realms. Earth is one realm. In a progression, we can gain access through the twelve heavens.

Of the thirty-three dimensions, each dimension can contain realms. The realms travel from dimension to dimension, while at the same time, that dimension gains increased access to higher realms and higher heavens, he explained.

To grasp this better, we asked for an example of how earth is a dimension that contains realms.

Just think of all the entities that exist. There are saints who are physically bound, but in the spirit, each has a realm and is inside a dimension.

However, do not think of a dimension as a natural plane.

We need a different understanding of it because it feels quantum and in time. It also feels stacked, layered, or encircled at the same time. Then, as these dimensions expand through trade (that is where the trade routes come in), the Kingdom of God, which is in the twelve heavens, expands also.

We and our dimension can expand or grow.

As it does, the realms inside that dimension have greater knowledge, understanding, access, and power, which comes from the levels of the heavens.

The realms inside the dimension help it to grow and fill its destiny scroll.

As the dimension grows, *those inside of it expand with their realms.* Not everyone has to do that at the same time though, because a remnant is always present. We will always have forerunners and pioneers. As they grow, it affects the dimension, so that the realms inside of it get an automatic increase, because it always takes someone to go first.

This is also connected to trade, as the realms inside the dimension trade in other dimensions and other realms.

This has been going on for a while, but we were unaware and, unfortunately, much has been co-opted by darkness. Humans and their realms have engaged illegally in trade. This means that things that are contrary to the will of the Father for certain things in other dimensions and the realms within those dimensions have occurred.

Light or Dark

Each dimension has both light and darkness. It is the plan of the Father for every dimension to become more light-filled (like on earth). This occurs through the saints and their expression of the Kingdom, or through the level of heavenly access they have been granted.

The pleasure of the Father (and all the other realms know this) is that because His Glory presence manifested in the form of Jesus in the earth realm, this dimension is marked for preeminence.

This dimension is marked for preeminence.

This means that someday it will reflect the fullness of the glory of all twelve heavens and its dimension will be changed. The heavens will be rolled back like an old garment,[7] and all other dimensions and their realms will trade with this new earth dimension[8] and its realms, because this is the way the Father planned it. This is how Jesus will receive all glory from every realm in every dimension. This is how the saints will steward the other dimensions, trading with all dimensions in that day.

Much later, in another engagement with Heaven where Malcolm was present and after we had received information on realms and dimensions regarding trade routes, I asked him to expound upon that for us.

Think of this grid (matrix) as the dimension. This is the dimension *and* the time. That is why they are important—why it is the important thing to do to have the angels go in time and out of time, and in every dimension. This is dimensional work. This is a dimensional trade. This is also the ancestral trade. This is quantum trade.

Referring to the grid or matrix, when our feet are on that initial ground that the Father has put us on, when a person on that grid decides to go another direction—as soon as they come off the Golden Path, all kinds of different dimensions open.

---

[7] Isaiah 34:4, Revelation 6:14
[8] Isaiah 65:17, Isaiah 66:22, 2 Peter 3:13, Revelation 21:1

Stephanie began describing what she was seeing, "I see a lot of different dimensions as if I am looking here in this direction and it's one color—it's like a portal—and I look in front of me and there is another completely different portal. I am looking down at my feet and there is a different one underneath me. They are all around. They are above, too! These are different timelines. These are different dimensions.

"If I took a step towards this that I see, Ron; it is like an upside-down triangle. That is what I see. Then the one next to it is right side up, all the way around. I see each one of them. It is like I can see landscapes in each one, and they are all assorted colors—so if I took a step forward into one, it takes me down an unusual pathway—a different pathway than the Golden Pathway on this grid."

These are different timelines, but are any of those the original path?

Once someone has agreed
to trade out of themselves,
there are many different pathways
in this system.

There are some that look terrifying.

Your word is a lamp to my feet and a light to my path. (Psalms 119:105)

That verse is so important and needs to be applicable. We had been seeing it as a Golden Pathway because it was *illuminated.*

If someone diverted from the path and the mistake is redeemed by repentance, it does not become a "new" Golden Path.

The Golden Path is never changed. It is in the center of the grid, with all the different choices all around us. If we step off this way or that way, that pathway is still there. Also, as we make good trades, a witness is present from the cloud of witnesses, and they witness the trade. We may also have an entity present; but *the intent of the cloud of witness is to turn us back towards the Golden Pathway.* It is always there for us.

How do we redeem a mistake of being diverted from the Golden Path?

By repentance—repentance is a trade. As a person repents, a man in white will help turn that person back towards the right path (because of a Godly trade that has been made in their behalf). Even though the pieces that were traded out of themselves into darkness and have been taken out of them—**once they get their feet back on the Golden Pathway, those pieces are restored to them.**

This is the agreement that we in Innocence made in the original plan of the Father. It is the agreement of the path that they agreed to with the Father. He is showing me this, as just one person, because every single person has a different agreement with the Father and has their own matrix to the left and to the right and behind them. But each has a pathway forward. Every person has their own destiny. This is about their own scrolls and their own destiny. It is the original plan between the Father and their Innocent self. The Father is calling us to that, and we have just been told about how to bring Innocence back.[9] That's why we came back to that Court of Trade, because it is from that court that all those pieces are restored. The grip of the enemy is no more. That is where the princes receive their eviction notices.

When princes get evicted, everything (in this case, an entity) that was in the house that belonged to the person is taken it out of the house and put on the curb. That is why, when the eviction comes, everything is put out.

The Godly trades, the innocence restored, the repentance, and the calling back of the fragmentations are what is bringing each piece back into that person as they are walking this path. It does not immediately happen, this restoration of themselves that they traded out of themselves—but it happens as they are walking on this path trading with Heaven. If, as we are walking and we sometimes step in poop, that is not getting us off to trade with the enemy—that is just stepping in poop. We can clean our shoes off and move on.

---

[9] See the segment on Pink Capture Bags in my book, *Dealing with Trusts and Consequential Liens in the Courts of Heaven*, LifeSpring Publishing (2022).

To move from the Golden Path is a decision that is made to walk and take a different path and trade out of ourselves into darkness. It is a rebellion.

The Scripture that says, "Rebellion is as the sin of witchcraft" is applicable, but the entire passage reads:

> *For rebellion is as the sin of witchcraft, and stubbornness is as iniquity and idolatry. Because you have rejected the word of the LORD, He also has rejected you from being king. (1 Samuel 15:23)*

That is why immediately when that person took that piece out of themselves and handed it to that entity, the demons came and walked with them in their realms. It is around *and* in them.

That is why so many Christians do not understand the difference between demonic possession and the demonic oppression. With demonic oppression, the demons are walking with us, influencing us. The adage of *who we surround ourselves with is who we become* speaks of this. Many have been taught that they cannot have a demon. The enemy has misconstrued this in religion on purpose to bring confusion and to make people say in and of themselves, "Well, I am not possessed. I do not have any demons." But if they traded into darkness and the oppression, the demonic walks with them. They have surrounded themselves with that.

Stephanie remembered hearing Pastor Robert Morris[10] who said that the first time he met James Robison,[11] he was trying to explain to him out of his Baptist mentality about being demonically oppressed. He said to James, "Well, do I have demons?" James answered saying, "Oh yeah, you have a whole flock of them." Pastor Morris, who was eating a bowl of ice cream at the time (he loves ice cream), said it is the first time in his entire life he couldn't—or he didn't—eat his bowl of ice cream. He related, "All I could think of was, 'I have demons! I have demons! Oh my God! I have demons!'" But it is so funny because this is an understanding that when we make that evil trade (to divert from the Golden Path), that is exactly what we get. Multiple demons come, walk with, and influence people when they divert from the Golden Path. But when we have the Godly trades, and we have witnesses that testify on our behalf, it is such a glorious thing.

Each of us are comprised of realms—the body realm, the soul realm, and the spirit realm. It is like three bubbles that are part of that person.

As a person trades into darkness, not all three realms are corrupted.

---

[10] Robert Morris is pastor of Gateway Church in Dallas-Fort Worth, Texas.
[11] James Robison is an evangelists and television host.

Usually just the soul and body realms are corrupted, but it could be the corruption of the body realm, the corruption of the soul realm, or the corruption of the spirit realm.

We can see in each of the realms where there has been a trade of someone's self into darkness. It takes a piece of that bubble, like the same exact piece, and we are seeing holes in each of the realms. It allows for those who, as they are walking along this path—even those that have been turned towards righteousness—it gives access to other things, including other imps and LHS's on assignment. Other beings have access to us.

We have seen how the bad works. We get it. It opens all three of our realms as we have traded out of ourselves into corruption. When we trade out of ourselves, parts get separated, corrupted, captured, and they get traded on. Darkness trades those pieces. The best way I can describe it is as if I take a piece of myself, I hand it off to darkness, and now I have this open place. Then they take that piece, and they trade on it, and they possibly trade it repeatedly.

Initially, this trade happens where they give the piece of themselves. After they have been on that route, that demonic entity closes that little shop down, and then goes and trades our pieces to other places. It is like we took our cell phone apart and sold the battery and the chips and the camera lenses to different people or places. It is like the entity has a little bag of people's parts, and he goes and trades them around.

If people understood, if they really understood who they are, and that part of their inheritance is understanding that they were in Innocence before the Father, before He created the earth and knew their value to Him—if people could grasp that they were present when He created earth, it would make such a difference.

Chapter 7
Paradigms

The entities Wisdom, Knowledge, and Understanding joined us in this upper conference room we were now in and took a seat at the table. Wisdom reminded us that we did not have to focus on how massive things appeared to us at times. As we looked down at the table, we saw the word "paradigms."

Wisdom explained to us that we are walking in a paradigm. There are many paradigms. There are Godly paradigms and ungodly ones. These paradigms are councils. This paradigm we are reading is a council. There are multiple paradigms and each of these paradigms is its own separate paradigm and there is a governing in each of them.

We must remember what is written in Joshua 24:15:

Choose you this day whom you will serve.

Scripture is a paradigm. It is a choice of a paradigm.

We had just learned about trading in and of ourselves into darkness. That is a paradigm. There are evil councils and wickedness that are set up that have created the routes with which each of our pieces of ourselves are traded on. There are other paradigms, and there is good in them. There is good, Godly counsel. They are strategic places upon the grid.

When there was a Godly trade, the witness (from the cloud of witnesses) then made trades in those Godly councils, the paradigms within paradigms. It is the same concept. Satan is a copycat. If Satan can trade pieces of us which are ungodly trades, then there are Godly trades made in and of ourselves as well.

A witness could have been somebody who knew us, a relative, or somebody that was aware of us that we did not know or anyone else Heaven assigned to us. Their role is at that place and time on the grid as a Godly trade is made. They go to this other paradigm, and it is like they are turning in that trade. It is recorded and put on the books. Then, from this Godly council of people, decisions are made related to that trade. It is like a decision-making process among them, to not only trade back into that person's life but to trade *greater things* back into that person's life.

> *There is a decision-making process among this counsel to not only trade back into our life, but to trade greater things back into our life because Heaven never does less.*

It is as if that man in white—that witness—took this piece of us and handed it over to the council and then they came back and said, "Heaven is giving this back to us bigger, much greater that the original piece...above all we could ask or think."[12]

As we looked down on the grid, we could see where there are places that the enemy had set up along the trade routes that we must give a piece of ourselves to keep going and moving forward down that path. There were places where these witnesses are set up for when we trade Godly things. The dominions of evil councils are set up above these places—above these Godly paradigms (it is as if it is a place, just like the ungodly is a place), but they are above. They are higher than these other paradigms.

It is not like a dominion. This paradigm is a place. It is a place, but it is just a different paradigm of a place. It is a strategic place that the Father put around this matrix where these Godly trades are made. That is why He is always bringing us back into Himself in a greater capacity—because even though we have traded into

---

[12] Ephesians 3:20

darkness, through the Godly trades that we have made, there is so much more given back to us.

> *Never doubt God's mighty power to work in you and accomplish all this. He will achieve infinitely more than your greatest request, your most unbelievable dream, and exceed your wildest imagination! He will outdo them all, for His miraculous power constantly energizes you. (Ephesians 3:20) (TPT)*

When we choose to trade with Heaven, pieces of our inheritance are brought back to us. When we choose to walk upon that original path, all our inheritance is laid before us.

That is what this means. As we walk on this path—remember, there were still pieces that were not all the way back—but as we are walking this out, those pieces are being brought back to us. The completion of that is the full inheritance. It is where we can tangibly see and experience the full inheritance that is ours, laid before us from the foundations of the earth. That is why the enemy fights so hard. They must fight harder because there is so much more stacked against them in the Godly trades.

There's so much more given back to us than what they take from us.

We have never been told that. That is why there has been hope deferred. People did not realize that, when they traded into the Kingdom of Heaven—even the simplest things—so much more is restored back to us. That is why the enemy fights so hard, because he does not have a leg to stand on. If we understood that victory, we would walk in this. There is no comparison to what the Kingdom of Heaven has in store for His people. That is why "greater is He that is in us than he that is in the world."[13]

> *So much more is traded back into us through Godly trades than what was traded out of us.*

Here is a simple example. We are walking along in our Christian life, and we slip up. We realize what we did and we repent immediately because we do not want anything between us and the Father. That is a Godly trade. What was meant to be taken out of us, that small bit of ourselves that we gave away for a moment—what is restored back to us is so much greater. People will not walk in the shame and be belittled by those mistakes that they have made—those mistakes made by those stepping off the path that they have made—when they realize so much greater is given back into them and to them from the Kingdom of Heaven, from these different paradigms, from these councils—because we have traded into Heaven.

That is why the Bible says that there is so much more for us and on behalf of us. There are so many more for

---

[13] 1 John 4:4

us than against us. We may have thought it was just the angels—it is not. Heaven has witnesses on our behalf. We have always heard and known that Jesus is our advocate. He is always praying on our behalf and interceding for us, but we also have these witnesses, too! We also have these Godly counsels that are trading back into us that are set up by the Father, and we have the angels. We also have those that are men and women in white that are from our family line. All these are interceding for us. There is so much greater for us than against us. Matthew 6:33 and the verses around it are examples of trade. As we seek the Kingdom, all these things (housing, clothing, food) are added.

Just as an individual person walking this out (and I do not walk in this anymore where I would just be so overcome with shame for the smallest thing that I did), people will not walk in that kind of tormenting shame because they understand how much more is being traded back into them than what they traded out of themselves.

———·———

Chapter 8
Understanding Realms

Our instructor for this encounter with Heaven was Malcolm. He wanted to give us an understanding of realms. I will summarize what he taught us.

Realms of Heaven are what we would call galactic or intergalactic. They are represented by spheres. Our spirit and our star are like this. The planet is like this, and the realms of Heaven can flow in and out of these spherical containers. They are many and varied. They each contain a flavor of the expression of God's knowledge, wisdom, power, and might. The Father and the Son, through the power of Holy Spirit, know all things in all realms from cycle to cycle. To understand this, we will need to consider the density of time. We will need to think of time as dense layers of cycles.

Imagine taking a slinky and putting its ends together, and what do we have? We have a spherical donut-shaped object with layers, each ring representing a layer. Now, imagine those rings are without end. Realize that realms are related to time, but it is easier to say that they are linked to time density. Some realms have yet to be opened, as they are reserved for other cycles. Some realms have been closed, having completed their revolution.

Building Realms

When we open the silver channel,[14] we are opening a passage to a realm.

When we build from creativity, we are building a realm because we are made like the Father, and we are an heir. Those made like the Father who are not heirs build realms of darkness, in league with total darkness. They capture things in those realms and therefore Satan needs them and is using them. He has convinced them through deception, but he holds them in bondage, some having given themselves over to him. Their realm has become not only dark, but a hollow, vast wasteland of nothing. This causes them to seek to deceive others, so that that they might capture another's realm.

This capturing of realms is what we see in satanic rituals. They use the soul, or the 3-D plane, to access the realm within the person. Therefore, they intentionally

---

[14] Opening the silver channel refers to one of the steps for releasing lingering human spirits. See *Lingering Human Spirits* by Dr. Ron M. Horner (LifeSpring Publishing) (2020).

fragment soul realms. They are seeking after the spirit realm that is connected to the soul realm.

To us, our realm is protected with the blood of Jesus and with angelic activity. It is protected with the Word of God and with righteous deeds. It is protected by a position that seeks to be filled by Holy Spirit, so that the clash of these realms in the density of time takes place.

There are many realms in our Father's Kingdom. Not all realms are available to us as natural, living beings. However, our spirit will eternally investigate realms, creating within the Father's massive realm His expression through us and through our spirit. Nations are also realms, having been built by a collective agreement.

Levels of Agreement Create Realms

Do we see how levels of agreement create levels of realms?

A neighborhood is a realm. A city is a realm. When two or more individuals agree, a realm is created—the individuals are filled with the agreement. This is what happened to Eve—she gave agreement to the one who coveted the realm she was responsible for stewarding. She had assignment to multiply. She came out of agreement with Adam and into agreement with darkness. This was a trade, and when other realms saw a human trade like this, it created illegal trading floors where they wondered at the centrality of Almighty God.

A portion of these other realms saw that they could trade with the offspring of the Father in illegal ways. This still goes on today. These illegal trading floors will be overthrown, and this is happening even now.

Stewarding Our Realm

We must steward our realm.

As we steward our realm with what we call the ways of the Father, we enlarge and empower it, and it becomes recognized by other realms. As we think larger, we begin to see an unlocking effect. Some realms only desire to trade with human realms that are filled with light because that realm is associated with the Most High. They are convinced of His centrality, meaning His Word is truth. He is who He is, as He told Moses. The statement, "I am that I am," was a signal to other realms, but it so filled Moses' realm with ability that he was able to accomplish what he did.

Many realms are watching this play out. Innumerable realms exist that we want to and can trade with.

*What people trade from
is an expression in their realm
of who the Father is.*

Those who are lacking the Father's light and the centrality of who He is—they trade from deception, control, bondage, and plunder. They trade what they have stolen from other realms because they have nothing good to trade. Right now, they are trading for our words. For this reason, we must speak the Word of God in season and out of season. Realms desire to trade off the words of the heirs of the Father.

———·———

Chapter 9
Trading Outside of Time

My Executive Assistant and I were scheduled to be guests on a podcast recently. Lydia (our heavenly Business Advisor) joined us and instructed us about the upcoming podcast. Heaven had downloaded insights into Commerce for Sons and Daughters of God which we shared at the initial podcast and ended that conversation with the statement, "And we haven't even talked about trading outside of time," (See the Preface). We were about to gain some insights into that with this engagement.

We were to talk about the practical components of operating from Heaven down™ with the audience. We started with talking about how, from Heaven down, those in Heaven (men and women in white, angels, and others) are primed and ready. They have already accepted assignments from the Father in the realms of Heaven—the eternal realms—so they are just waiting on those on the earth. They are not twiddling their thumbs waiting, but they are waiting for any who will come and shrug off religious paradigms that prevent the access of heavenly revelation.

It is a combination of belief that we have an invitation to trade from Heaven down to engage Heaven's input for our trade, to access hidden wealth, wisdom, functionality, creativity, and nuances of relational ideas that come from Heaven that are quite easy to follow through with on earth.

We started with talking about operating from Heaven down once we have documentation (our Declaration of Trade and the Deed of Commerce and Trade), and a beginning relationship with those assigned to us from Heaven for our business/ministry. Heaven is always ready.

The men and women in white are quite ready to do this. Heaven is waiting on us. They are waiting for those who bravely launch and try.

When our child or grandchild is learning to walk, and they fall over after two toddling steps, we do not get upset if they fall. We are excited that they are trying.

Heaven is fully invested in our toddling steps. They are primed to help us. They are never disappointed. They are happy with our effort, and our desire to understand this way of doing business from Heaven down™. This is the way it has always been meant to be with the sons and daughters of God. Heaven has so much to share, and all that Heaven must share comes from Father.

> *Everything Heaven shares comes from the vast warehouses of the Father's ability, creativity, provision, etc.*

Since Father is always creating Himself, then Heaven wants to help His sons and daughters with the new.

Heaven may not necessarily be aiming to talk to us about the old. They will talk about what can be and what should be. God's people and Heaven creating the future together is one of the plans of the Father. Doing this from trade—which is taking something and multiplying it—is ideally suited for this.

Know that the enemy wants to corrupt what we have determined to believe. Until the day of the Lord, the corruption of his character will remain. He will operate from the corruption of his character until then.

> *The child of God focused on Heaven does not have time to worry about Satan's mess because we are so engaged in putting into practice and operating from the design of Heaven.*

Some call these the blueprints of Heaven. Some call these the will of Heaven. Some call these the negotiations of Heavenly realms through the portals, which are the sons and daughters of God, so that the earth becomes a reflection of Heaven. This is the plan of the Father and these plans do NOT fail.

The Fabric of Time

Time is like fabric and malleable from the spirit realm. When we step into spiritual places, the time fabric is different. It does not move or sway like we are accustomed to on earth. It is unsettling at first to recognize that...

---
*From eternal realms
all things are possible.*

Reaching back in time, reaching forward in time, bringing time together, or the melding of time is possible here. Of course, it would be, but we must learn not to be freaked out by this.

---
*Discipline the soul
to receive that this is possible.*

Do not consider it odd or off limits because it is not!

Access has been granted.

How will sons and daughters of God grow in these things if they do not come to the heavenly realms and try? If they do not embrace what manner of depth that exists in heavenly places?

Here is a motivator—our enemy and principalities and powers of darkness have been trying to do this for a long time.

When we understand that those who are trying to operate in the occult, which is illegal access to Heavenly realms, illegal access to what God has reserved for sons and daughters of the King—if they value it enough to try to steal it, it must be valuable.

Why are we not trying to come in and understand how time works, or lack of time, or how time is malleable in different dimensions? We should absolutely understand that our Father created it all. He created the eternal realm, which is the 'not time' realm, and He created the time realm for sons and daughters of God.

We are like Jesus in this and can operate in and out of time.

This should not be a surprise. It should not freak us out, and if it does, we are still trapped by religious paradigms.

Religion will keep us from our inheritance. The religious find their comfort in ritual. The spirit of religion behind religiousness is wicked, because it wants to box in and prevent access to all that the Father has made available to His sons and daughters.

> *It is the Father's good pleasure to give you the Kingdom. (Luke 12:32)*

This verse is the invitation—the proof text of the Father's willingness to work with those who will step into heavenly realms by faith, with belief, and trade from there.

> *Abraham did this;*
> *he traded out of time!*

He traded out of time for the purpose of the heir. His request was so firm, and he was so firm in his understanding, that even as a man of time he could wait inside of time for the fulfillment.

What we see in his life's story are the interruptions of demonic temptations and his struggle to remain firm in faith regarding the trade that he knew he had made. Abraham knew this trade was not initiated by himself—this trade was initiated by Heaven.

Trading Outside of Time

How do we trade outside of time?

> *First, understand that faith*
> *is the currency of the trade.*

The trade is both spiritual and eternal—it is outside the dimension of time. It is outside of the dimension of the 3-D plane. It must be engaged in by our spirit. Our soul cannot trade outside of time. It cannot trade with Heaven. Our spirit trades with Heaven. Our soul cannot be involved.

*All things transfer **through** the spirit realm using the currency of faith for the manifestation of what we have believed for.*

Attempts have been made in some areas that were very infantile, but notice Heaven is not upset with those who tried. Some simply ran ahead without wisdom. They ran ahead without understanding. They ran ahead without counsel and were not even crawling yet. They were still infants lying on their back. But just because the attempts were infantile, Heaven does not close the door to it. The access is still open. It has just been a momentary need for the Body of Christ to have time to mature and come alongside.

We are as righteous sons and daughters of God in Jesus Christ. We are to seek first that Kingdom, that King's domain, the King's realm, the Kingdom inside the King's realm, and the King inside.

Inside the King's realm is the King's heart.

We must mature and learn the ways of this King's realm.

Unrighteous activity, deeds of darkness, and manipulation (being motivated by control to rule over others by way of gaining identity) is not the King's way.

When we seek to grow up in this area, Holy Spirit is the teacher and counselor. The need of the son or daughter of God is to pay attention and be willing to surrender and be schooled by the Spirit of God within.

Trouble happens when the unction of Holy Spirit is ignored.

And when all the signs are being displayed by the hands of angels to assist the saint in remaining free of temptation and the will of Heaven is ignored, this is when trouble for the saint begins. The grace of Heaven comes into play at the point of repentance, for that son or daughter is never lost to the Father, being in the covenant blood of Jesus. But the blessing may be lost until repentance is sought and we gain a willingness to play out the role that we have been given and not another's role.

For example, the son is not the father, the father is the father.

Corruption comes when the son tries to be the father.

We can take this either from natural or spiritual understandings. The same is true.

Frustration with World Systems

I am speaking to the sons and daughters who have a deep current riding within them that causes their frustration with world systems. Those who are aware of the intensity of the dissatisfaction with world systems, to these very sons and daughters of God is given the invitation to bring forth what Heaven has as the alternative to world systems.

---
*Do not expect the world system
to run to our door when we are
bringing something from Heaven.*

A lot of spiritual establishment must take place before those who have been lured by world systems will turn their face to encounter the jewel that we have mined from Heaven and are now presenting as an alternative.

Yet, there are many names on many scrolls that *are* embracing the jewel we have mined from Heaven. Our stewardship of that jewel will be to not expect the world systems to give us honor or recognition for it, for those remain for us in heavenly places.

> *Some of this is a surrendering to the point of willingness to turn one's back on world systems and their measured ranking of recognition.*

Yet, there are scrolls written about this in Heaven that have already been opened and are being read by us here in eternal realms, and now, our true excitement grows! This new opening of intensity for the sons and daughters of God to throw off shackles of identity from world systems, forsaking that for what has been stored up in heavenly places for them outside of time—

> *To these sons and daughters are given the invitation to bring forth what Heaven has as the alternative to world systems.*

We have a saying: "If one life is changed, it is worth the doing." Equate this to the Scripture where it says Jesus would leave the ninety-nine to find the one sheep[15]—not lost as in salvation, but lost as in having lost its path to be shepherded by the Good Shepherd.

> *Jesus was making trade by being a shepherd.*

---

[15] Matthew 18:13

And He does it well. He does it with excellence.

Do we see the new measuring of what we would deem or term success? Do we see that the new measuring of Heaven must be engaged once again?

The soul is not suited for this, but the spirit is because it has capacity to gain spirit knowledge.

This is a satisfaction of the spirit of a man or woman.

All things are not profitable, but all things are possible.

---

*Discernment from our oneness with the Spirit of the Lord and all His seven refractions[16] **will equate** to Heaven's success through our portal.*

One of the pitfalls is where we measure by emotional terms from the soul realm that which should be measured by the spirit. This sets a disharmony and dissonance within the vessel—the body of the person. It is simply because the soul is trying to do the job of the spirit, or the soul is out of alignment where life from the

---

[16] Referring to the Seven Spirits of God found in Isaiah 11:2.

inner man should triumph even over life from the soul. Is this not the final triumph?

———·———

Chapter 10

Trading on Ungodly Bonds

A current global crisis was on our minds when Eric (a man in white who was tutoring us) came to give us instruction.

The realm of darkness is engaged in ungodly bonds, and they are trading on them. Some ungodly bonds come from the soulish actions of people, others from the courts of hell, and still others from galactic interference.

Imagine an entity—a galactic being—who is trading on the power of how many ungodly bonds they have released against the sons of God. They do not receive power directly from the person they have put the bond on. That ungodly realm has a sort of scale that gives them knowledge of that. They can tell. They search out the counsels of hell. They search out legalities. The bond can be iniquities in the bloodlines and things like that. The searching out of those is to continue to put the bonds on the living, which is the work of darkness. These galactic beings get recognized for however many ungodly bonds are successfully applied.

This is what makes the courtrooms of Heaven revelation so imperative for the sons of God to realize that they have access to remove the legal grounds, because the enemy is using the legal grounds against the saints. That realm is somehow able to recognize those who have studied and found loopholes and devious ways to even trip the saints up so that they can bring charges and have legal grounds to then implant an ungodly bond.

The power that came to the ungodly is not the power the person has that the enemy put the bond on, but the ungodly power they would gain out of the ability to affect the numbers of people through the impact of that ungodly bond. That power could be applied and works generationally through several people living on the earth. Let's say we have a person in India and an ungodly bond is loosed against a man, his community, and however many places that his life touches (which is going to exponentially increase)—to afflict a man who has a lot of sway in a community would grant the being more power. The more influence the recipient has, the more power is derived from placing the ungodly bond. It would be important to trip up a major leader in the Body of Christ.

A person's sphere of influence, a person's following (that would also be their sphere of influence), and even a person's family lines are involved. Imagine Celebrity A marries Celebrity B, and the influence of that one celebrity to the other cross-germinates, so influence is multiplied. They would get more brownie points for that kind of big score.

Height and width were mentioned, and we wondered what that meant. It was explained to us as the height of a person's status and the width of their reach—but do not let that confuse us that the councils of hell are not also searching out the grandmother who prays in her house constantly and has little influence or power—they work to stop both.

Imagine a grandmother like that praying in her living room but operating in the courts to remove the bonds, not only from herself but from others as well—what a powerhouse she is, what a hidden fire she is.

We had a sense that the bonds that were on the galactic level were on a different plane than the bonds we have been dealing with typically.

We have dealt with the demonic principalities and powers, but on occasion we end up dealing with galactic entities or a galactic prince. They are the ones responsible for the high-tech tracking devices that are not an average run of the mill tracking device. They have a bond that seemed to go on a different level. That was the inference to us. We had been coming across that often. This would fall into the category of other realms—bonds from other realms. This is the essence of the dirty trade and the other realm beings are interested in working with spirits assigned against the earth. The galactic beings do not want to get their hands dirty, so they are working like hidden slave masters behind the curtain, and they are employing others to do the work for them. My sense of this is these beings are separate from our low-level demons, but they feel more intelligent. We have our low-level demon who works for a boss, right? And then that boss works for a boss, correct? Those are all earthbound earth realm evil beings, but the beings behind the curtain are these galactic beings that are employing the bosses that work the demons as slaves—it is like that.

The intensity level of the evil here is increased exponentially. It is vastly increased, and these evil beings have divided themselves into leagues and there is a great competition among these leagues to gain influence and power in the running of the evil realm and the evil spirit/low level demons.

Prince Pretenders

For instance, a low-level demon manages to trip up a person of profound influence. Then he brings that to the boss and that boss brings it to his boss. The earth-realm principality boss then takes that to the galactic being. The galactic being, along with his league (since that is related to his realm), is empowered by that trade and that translates to the fact that he now has more status against the other leagues. They are prince pretenders, also known as princes of the power of the air.

We asked about the removal of these bonds—can we do so in the same way or is there a different location for those records? Heaven told us that we would need greater access for that, so we asked if it would require a key or a badge, or if we could simply request access. We were told it was a matter of timing. If we run into this when doing bond work, just keep doing the bond severance the way we have been taught.

The bond severance that we have been taught—the spread of it and the use of it by the saints, especially the use of it over cities—is so young still that it needs to have time to grow. We must have more embracing of this revelation by the saints. We must have more engagement of the severance of bonds. Remember individual, family, city, nations—it must mushroom. It must grow. It must be more seeded into the earth realm. As we do that, the gained power of these prince pretenders and the power they have been given is redeemed. There will come a day where the next level of bond severance is open to the saints, but that has not happened yet.[17]

Do not think it's a linear thing; just work so that we are approved as a good workman and can continue in the task until that day.

---

[17] At the time we received this revelation, the information covered in *Dealing with Trusts & Consequential Liens in the Courts of Heaven* had not been unveiled. LifeSpring Publishing (2022).

Transition of Trade

In a vision, a giant ship could be seen which we understood that the ship represents a trade route. In the vision, the ship was Phoenician. We were seeing it because what we are undergoing in the current day is a transition of trade. The populations of the earth right now, due to Coronavirus, have been under duress, a transition of trade.

A person in white whose name we were not given came forth and explained that he operates in the merchant area of the Business Complex. He explained that the ship was in reference to transition of trade.

Nations are created to trade. Their population within the nations itself is created to trade on many levels of trading. The unseen realm works through trade as well. The profaning of trade was sin. When we profane trade at certain levels, it corrupts purpose and destiny. Trade routes are being traded in galactic areas right now.

The trade routes themselves are up for auction in the earth, which is why the earth is experiencing this. We were told that Coronavirus is being used as a tool to implement this. This is against the will of the Father and outside of the timing of Heaven. Satan is trying to change times and seasons.

Trade routes and all their many dimensions are synchronized with the time of the Lord, like in the days of Nebuchadnezzar. Nebuchadnezzar had reached a pinnacle point in the control of trade, which began to corrupt him and for which he paid dearly. This was related to Babylon—it was premature. Nebuchadnezzar was like a pawn to galactic entities trying to make trade route changes that had not been approved by the Father.

We would have to look between the lines to see this in Scripture, but it is there. Remember the statute that Daniel saw. Each of those markers of time were other attempts at violation of trade routes, and they are trading off their bluffing. It is like at a poker table, when one person says, "I have this," and the other guy says, "Maybe you do." It is not a pleasant, honest activity that they hope to engage in one day. These beings will use humans or spirits. They will use the interplay of their spirit realm society's maneuverings. They have been doing this since ancient times.

Their goal is the earth and to dominate humanity.

Chapter 11
Understanding Trade Routes

Continuing from the prior engagement, we asked our instructor, Osirus, if he could assist us at the basic level to understand trade routes—the galactic trade routes that we saw—the pathways in the heavens that went into the earth.

There are some things we cannot understand, just as Jesus told the disciples. We *can* know that there are hidden trade routes that intersect dimensions of the earth realm of which we are not aware. These trades have been ongoing. We must broaden our mind to understand the largeness of the Creator and the differing realms and beings.

The goal of trade is power.

The goal of trade is not authority, it is power. It is like illegal power; in a phrase, we would call that demonic power. They do not refer to it like that because it is not that race of being, but it is a pursuit of power. They know they cannot pursue authority.

---

*What they are doing
is pursuing power
outside of authority,
and that makes it illegal.*

---

*A purpose of a demonic trade
is to "one up you."*

Essentially, they say, "I am not going to ever trade righteously with you. I am always going to trade with my thumb on the scale. I am always going to seek to outdo you to get a bargain over you—get a one up on you." Acting in that manner gives them something like bragging rights when they can prove to other galactic beings that that is what we have engaged in and successfully done.

We must imagine a realm completely without righteousness, completely operating in the dark, completely content to operate that way. But it is unrighteousness—wickedness at every turn. It is like wickedness trying to outdo wickedness, evil trying to outdo evil. The redemption—the redemptive work of the saints—is to the Godhead; it is for the eventual overturn of every wicked realm, beginning with the earth but moving into other realms. In the natural, we have seen wickedness in human history, but we have not connected the dot—that there are those operating like that and who are being moved by these galactic leagues that are competing against each other for power. This like a giant board game to those beings.

The resultant authority given to the sons of God and those sons operating in their authority—as they grow up in the church, and by that, is meant as the Bride—she herself gains more of her own authority and moves in it. I am talking about collective, large group unity movements. We do not have those yet, but eventually we will. It will, at one point, cause the heavens to unroll—mentioned in that verse in Revelation.

Why is the earth the goal?

Because the Father has decided that He will marry the earth realm with the realm of His Kingdom, in revealing the overlay of his Kingdom, He has divinely chosen to do so through the creation of the earth. Thus, the earth is the point of contention. It is the goal. It is the prize. Thus, to Adam, He said, "Subdue the earth" and in subduing, He meant to steward it before the Lord so that it could become the Kingdom of Heaven on earth—that is our basics.

We can look at it like this: these galactic players gain power by causing misery and by wooing the human sons of man (not the sons of God but the human sons of men), luring them and tempting them into agreement with their evil agendas. Thereby, they take that human who thinks he has all this power, but really, he is a pawn and is being used by these galactic players.

Many of the humans are finding unnaturally long life due to the powers given to them to from these galactic beings. Because the humans are still living, the beings have need of their carcass. The galactic beings, because they are not human—they are spirit beings of some type—so these galactic beings must have a point of contact. They must have a human to carry out what their goal is.

Reptillians

Some of these individuals will manifest as reptillians.[18] Over time, a human engaged in this sort of endeavor eventually surrenders their life to that entity, that galactic partner. Imagine the covenant they are engaged in—that is an evil covenant. They are engaged in evil worship. Rituals and all those activities are a form of evil worship, but the more a person is engaged in that, the more they give themselves over to it and the deeper the darkness that they are engaged in. We know how, as the sons of God, we died in Christ and were raised in Him—it is the same way with the dark side, where, when they die, they give their life away, and they are promised covenant promises from that evil side. We can think of it

---

[18] Refers to those who shape shift from human to reptile-like.

as a total mirror of the other side of that. They eventually lose their life, and that entity can take over.

This reptilian scenario is only one league or type of player the galactic beings use. Humans cannot take the full amount of transformation required, because then that carcass would no longer be human. It is a delicate interplay of how much they can get away with until that carcass is no longer human, but the minute they cross that line, they lose all their power. They are hybrids of a sort.

There are other races of beings that exist on the interplay of dimensions, but all these interplays of dimensions have access to earth. Should they choose to engage with earth, they could. Many in ancient times have done so. Many have decided earth is not worth that right now. They are not engaging in the earth realm, in the dimensional field, or in the plane that would be the portal opening between their realm and earth.

The sons of men are not meant to redeem all of these—not the demonic, not the league players, but the other races. They are to trade with them those races. Concerning the Father's race of humans, it was the divine will to come as the Godman through Jesus to redeem sons to Himself for the purpose of those sons to redeem all races—even races we do not know about right now—at least to play a part in that and to play a part in the judging of the nations. But it is not nations in the sense of geography as much as it is judging of the races. It is judging of the DNAs, if we could say it that way. It is the different races being redeemed to the Creator through the sons of God who are in connection with Jesus, operating in oneness with Him.

Our instructor then gave us an example using the science fiction movie series *Star Trek* saying, "You know how, in the recent feature film movies, where the aim of the intergalactic council was to go out and explore, and usually, what they did find was a race in need? In their humanity, they helped them out and helped things come to some resolution, and the counsel that sent them out was trying to befriend them so that a trade happens. This may not be real *Star Trek*, but this is what I am saying. If the sons of God or that council work with the court realms of Heaven, then redemption is possible.

We always have the legal means through the Courts of Heaven to bring all things back to Him.

"All things that want to remain out of alignment with Him, the sons of God are given the opportunity to bring into alignment, by the working out of the courts, and the grace and the mercy that they would extend to a race, because they are working in their Father's business. Think of it like that. We could say in a future era or in a future age, an age to come, that is what the contention is going to land on. The point of the final war is going to be on the earth because this is where we are."

And the evil side of that? That is what the plan of the Father is for—His sons to operate in, briefly, doing the work of redemption back to the Father. If the sons of God are employed in the work of redemption everywhere they go, redeeming things back to the Father, back to alignment, back to rightness with Him—then the work of those who have chosen to stand as enemies against God are doing the exact same thing, only from the dark side. Since they do not have what the sons of God have, they have only to spy on them, trip them up, bring them into temptation, and all of that. The dark side is hoping against humanity understanding that the Father is reaching out to them to afford them a way they can get freed of the shackles they find themselves in. That is just a unique way of saying the gospel, isn't it?

On the earth we have all the different races of men, and so the Star Trek Federation thing is trying to give us a picture of what we are about. They are always going on peacekeeping missions to other solar systems and to other planets.

Think about how we have a family. We want to redeem our family first, right? We want to see it all go well with our family, right?

Think of it like this: in the terms of the Father, He wants to see His family—He wants to see that it will be right with the earth, this first planet. But what this planet does not realize is there are all these other outside races affecting what the Father is trying to do with His family.

We are told to go to the city, the state, the county, and all the different levels. But where does it have to start? It starts first in my house, then my community, then, I must have my state running well. These are the various roles of the sons of God, even to nation states and then to races, and the sons of God need to know the timeframe to do that. This is part of the broadening ability of the church as the Bride grows up.

It is not that we are still young, it's just that we have a way to go. But do not to think linearly because with exponential growth, it mushrooms. Therefore, the understanding of the era is important.

The Father is content that not all members have to be awakened. That is why we cannot disparage the other people in the Bride. They are just not awakened yet, but they will be. There are tares[19] too.

Not every church is a church that the Father built.

One of the league's agendas is to find a remnant in the earth that is *neutral to God* and *open*. They are not evil. They have not fallen into the pit of evil. They are not shackled to rituals and all of that, but they are not hot for God, either. They are in this middle of the road, and the aim is to create a larger population that is in the middle of the road, because they can do something with that. They can sway that population. Therefore, Father said, "Be hot or cold, don't be lukewarm."[20]

---

[19] Tares are weedy plants that grow in fields of grain.
[20] Revelation 3:16

Creating Neutral Populations

The agenda of the leagues is to create a populous so neutral that their conscience is seared to God. They no longer have a moral compass, or they do not have a compass at all, so they wander. A wandering populace, if a nation falls into that, is a preferred state according to these leagues—like in the days of Noah with everyone turning to his own way, doing his own thing—where everyone is doing according to their own way.

---

*A populace neutral to God
is available for trade.*

These are the souls of men whose souls are seared; a seared soul is not evil. It is not like they are hot to serve. They have been marked neutral and, if they are marked neutral, it equates to "they do not have to worry about these people." They become the subject of the trade.

The cares of this world and things like that will cause us to be neutral to God and cause us to forget whose likeness we are made in.

Let's say a league of beings is working through a particular nation to bring it to a neutral state—then they gain power from that in their world and in their realm, so they can trade on that. It somehow gives them power to trade. It almost becomes like there is not an actual thing that they trade, it is just this power marker.

As we were receiving these insights, we paused to reflect on how we were having to let some old concepts (or misconceptions) go and embrace new concepts. Readers may be facing the same thing.

As we see the galactic leagues trading for these neutral populations, there must be a redemptive way to bring about the opposite result. The trade is unto God as we redeem them for Him. Regarding these neutral ones, we begin rescuing them, showing them how to become disciplined and not to be neutral.

If we did a word study in Scripture about neutrality and all the different things Jesus said—all the different positive things He said about keeping our fire burning, keeping our heart hot for God—those things are instructions about how not to fall into this neutral state. The fear of mankind falling into the neutral state is their deceit. That is their deception.

The goal of these galactic leagues is to bring more of the populace to neutrality.

Their purpose is to bring back to God this amount of the population made in Father's image who are no longer hot, pursuing after God. Once the population is neutral to God, the galactic leagues want to then force His legal hand (for they know Who rules in righteousness and justice). Their attempt to force the legal hand is to make Him give up the earth, to give up His own creation, to give them over. But then they will never win. That is their deception. He is God, and they are not. They are created beings.

Satan knows they cannot gain more glory than God. He already tried that and failed. What he can gain, though, is he can take those that would worship God and make them neutral. He can then present God with a package that says, "This many on the earth are neutral. They are neither for me, nor are they for You." Therefore, the accusation against God is that "God has lost power, and Satan has gained power," because of the amount of neutrality in the earth of the sons of men. The playing out of this is of a scope our instructor could not see and understand.

Satan does know what his ultimate end is, and he knows it more than we do. He understands it at a greater depth than we do, but that does not mean he is not working overtime. This is where the nation of Israel, those who are born after the bloodline of Abraham, come in; it is the trump card that we always will use against Satan's argument because the Father will turn the hearts of the fathers to the children and the children to the fathers.[21] He will create a fire in that nation and by nation He means genetic bloodline—Israel. He will fulfill His promise to Abraham and to David.

Resisting Neutrality

Remember, Scripture tells us that God knows the heart. The heart reveals the degree of heat for God, the passion for God—for the Father—and it is made up of

---

[21] Malachi 4:6

that heat for God. Many things contribute to the loss of passion, including the bloodline. The curse on a person is from the iniquities of that bloodline. Thus, the work of the cleansing of bloodlines is to give people a fighting chance—not to fall into neutrality, but to continue to have the ember of God in them burn after the Creator and yearn for God. When Adam fell and lost his glory covering, he lost the yearning of his heart to know God. Even in his fallen state, the degree of glory that was still at work because the glory had previously been on him was so powerful that the Father could meet with him even after he was released from the garden of Eden.

The memory of Adam's blood still held the quantity of the memory of the Glory, therefore, God could still meet with him and talk to him. Therefore, Cain and Abel were able to talk to God and to commune with God. For that reason, they knew what worship of the Father was. The battle would then be over the territory of man's heart, but it's not really territory. Mostly, it is the needle of that man's heart and belief system—his conscience.

Chapter 12
The Harvest of Trade

As Stephanie and I engaged Heaven, we wanted to learn more about the subject of trade and trading floors. As we stepped into Heaven, we found Malcom leaning on a fence post on the edge of a massive wheat field. He had a stalk of wheat hanging out of his mouth. He turned around and showed us all the harvest. It was massive and glorious.

The color of the wheat was so golden and there were so many stalks of it. When people drive by a wheat field, they do not even realize how close each piece of wheat comes up next to the other. We did not see any tares in this wheat, either.

The question we were asked was, "Do we trust to trade?" We answered affirmatively and continued walking.

We continued walking until we came to a large multi-story building. The walls were made of glass, allowing us to see through them. There were six or seven floors, and we could see that a lot was going on inside the building. We noticed how huge this complex was, and surrounding the building was wheat. We walked down the pathway to the front entrance and went through the doors to the one of the two desks in the lobby. It had a glorious stone floor—it was not diamond, though it was exquisite. It was white like pearl.

The walls were made of glass and each individual office was also walled in glass. There was an individual in each office, but people were coming in and out of these offices doing work. Stephanie went to the desk on the left and was greeted by a woman in white named Francis who had short black hair. Francis came around to the front of the desk. At this point, Malcolm passed us off to Francis.

We all got on an escalator, came to the second floor, and went to the right. Stephanie could see individual desks throughout the room with people working behind them. We continued walking, came to the end of a hallway, and took another right turn. We came to a large open floor with a lot of open space with one desk and two side chairs.

Francis informed us we already had a meeting scheduled on the books at this desk. A man was sitting behind the desk named Jackson. Jackson turned his chair to the side and moved out of our view. All we could see was fields of wheat.

Jackson explained that what we were seeing represented the harvest—the harvest that is here and now. The harvest that has come. This is the stewardship that I took as I gave ownership to Jesus. It reminded me of the Bible story that Jesus told about the master that left the coins in the different people's care (the parable of the talents). I had been the one that had taken the greatest care with what the Father has given me—a small piece of trade.

As we were talking, he took a small token (that looked like a coin) and handed it to me and said, "I have given you this little coin, which represents the information and revelation that you, Ron, have received. Heaven traded it into you, and you have taken it and been a good steward and multiplied it."

He turned around and was sitting in front of us. He began to show Stephanie what looked like shares and explained that my stewardship has created an ownership in the business of Heaven. He said, "This is what a good trade produces."

When people trade with us to purchase a book, and then they disseminate the information they have received, they are trading again, which is creating dividends. In front of us, it looked as if I had ownership and stock in the company, which is what this is.

Many people have been brought up with the knowledge that doing good deeds for people is sowing. That is why we see the harvest. There is a time for sowing and there is a time for reaping, but the gains are so much better than we could have ever thought. Trading in Heaven brings wealth to great proportions, not just wealth as in money, but wealth in the richness and the riches of Heaven.

Fruits of the Spirit

As we pray, the Fruit of the Spirit increases in us. Just being a good person towards somebody is a type of trade. When we took those actions of goodness and were a good steward of them, it created this multiplication, this dividend. The understanding is that the people can have this same opportunity in trading with Heaven.

Knowledge is a trade. As we teach the truth about the Kingdom of Heaven and the principles behind it, the Kingdom of Heaven is at hand for people to gain knowledge of the Courts of Heaven. When the people begin trading with Heaven, then their knowledge of the Kingdom of Heaven grows exponentially. It creates a Kingdom Dynamic of the Father and the harvest that is coming—the harvest that is here. It is now ripe.

Stepping into Heaven is a trade. We are trading by leaving our soul and our body behind and stepping into a realm that is not available in the earth realm. We are trading belief for unbelief because the Kingdom of Heaven is here now!

Worship is a trade. Generational cleansing is a trade with great harvest. Repentance is a trade.

When the Senior Advocates and Junior Advocates day in and day out step out of themselves and step into

Heaven on behalf of someone else, that is a trade. They are laying down their life for another. It is a gift from themselves that they are giving to a person. That is a trade in a natural world, but it is also creating a trade in Heaven, and there is a huge multiplication benefit of that.

The intercessors are trading with Heaven. When they trade their time to do this intercessory work on their day, then that time is going to be traded back to them.

Those that have traded to be in CourtsNet[22] are trading with Heaven. This is a type of trade and is not just with LifeSpring but with Heaven and coming to agreement with the realities of Heaven. It creates a trade.

When someone goes to sell their stock and they reap the reward, they are not really selling their shares—they are just recouping the benefit. They can come and freely ask for them because they have said "yes" to Heaven, because they are trading *with* Heaven. Because they are doing these things, and they are acting as trades, they can step into this place. This is a part of the Hall of Commerce. Yet, this is greater than that. There is no repentance because this is a trade with Heaven. These are Godly things done in and of themselves with Heaven, with the Father because of the Son.

The huge amount of wheat we had seen that angels were out harvesting is not the harvest of people coming to the ministry, but it is the harvest of those that trade

---

[22] CourtsNet is our online video training.

with Heaven. The harvest is stored in the storehouses of Heaven, and we can commission the angels to bring Godly trades to us and to our realms from those storehouses. This well pleases the Father. It is a pouring out of the abundances of Heaven, as people begin to understand that their trading with Heaven has reaped great reward and that they can ask for those rewards. It is bursting at the seams.

The more trade occurs, the more sowing and reaping results.

But the sowing and reaping is on a much greater level than we had previously imagined.

The simple interactions that we have with our videos and our tools—these are trades. There is great benefit and wealth in that we are given a wealth of knowledge. Then, we are taking that knowledge and giving it to the people, and they are gaining a wealth of knowledge. Every time that trade is made to another person, as soon as it is made, it leaps over to that person. There is a leaping back into the storehouses of trade and then each person tells another person, and there is a residual harvesting coming back to the storehouses.

This is enacted because of the laying down of strongholds, the laying down of old mindsets, the laying down of religious thinking. On behalf of the people in the warehouses, they have full access as they walk in this more—so did Jesus when He was here, and He was talking about this. He already saw this in Heaven and understood this—these storehouses—the sowing and reaping.

The Flip Side

We also have what happens in the evil kingdom. As we do evil, evil is stored in their storehouses and warehouses, and that is automatically released upon us. This is the concept in hell. The sowing and reaping of hell is *ugly*.

By simply sowing a minor infliction by being mean to somebody or saying something mean to somebody, it comes back as torment to the sower. When someone trades a word of gossip, a beast is released to torment.

The concept of trading with Heaven was set up at the foundations of the earth. This is the Father's Kingdom promise to the earth and how all these things shall be added unto us (Matthew 6:33).

———·———

Chapter 13
The Hall of Commerce

The large room Stephanie and I entered contained a lot of people and a lot of activity in the room. It reminded us of a trading floor. It was called the Halls of Commerce. Remarkable things were in store for us.

This is the abundance of Heaven. This is the righteous trading floor of the people, just like in the natural commerce we see and experience. There is commerce in Heaven.

When we rightly divide the truth, when we understand the realities that Heaven is a trade and people rightly divide the truth about that, commerce is available. The commerce of Heaven includes the goodness of God, the flow, the value, and the frequency. Understanding and Wisdom trade here with the people on behalf of them. This is one of the great unknowns to most—that there is value on the trading floors of Heaven. When people press in, when people choose to trade with

Heaven, trade with the Father, trade with Wisdom and Understanding, there can be great exploits for the sons.

How Heaven wants us to trade is bigger than just through tithes and offerings.

Within the confines of the space, we were seeing there were a lot of small offices around what would be the perimeter of the space. We saw men and women in white going to the center of the space, collecting paperwork, and then bringing it to the offices around the edges of the Hall of Commerce.

It was explained that we were seeing a portal where this trade happens in the hearts and minds of people. It is where decisions are made to trade the commerce of Heaven—the goods of Heaven—as sons.

When they realize the true nature of being a son, all the goods of Heaven are accessible. This trading route is larger and bigger than most could comprehend. It is the favor of the Father, exceedingly and abundantly above what we could ask or think.[23]

Think of it like this: there are goods and services in the earth realm that people see seek out and trade with. There are goods and services in Heaven. Remember types and shadows—that is what the earth is. It is a type and shadow of what the reality is in Heaven. As sons, we have full access of the Godly trades of Heaven.

---

[23] Ephesians 3:20

We may only see it as one giant portal, but everyone can trade through that with their decision and their mindset to trade on the trading floors of Heaven for goods and services of what Heaven brings into people's lives. It is so much bigger than what we could think or imagine. That is what the Father wants people to know. He is so much bigger than what we could think or imagine, and we can trade upon that thought process and that love that He has. We could not even imagine the things that He has for us, the things He is going to give us when we trade with Him—when we choose, and it *is* a choice.

The goods of Heaven, the Fruits of the Spirit, can be easily attained here in Heaven. People have assumed that they are supposed to pull those Fruits of the Spirit out of themselves to trade here. It is what the Father brings to their hearts: goodness, kindness, gentleness, mercy, and self-control—it can be given from Heaven.

What did Jesus do when He was on the earth? He served. The trades from here will cause people to want to desire what He did, which was to serve others. That is the truest form of love.

The largest trade here is love.
Love abounds in this place.

We can step into this portal—this place. We can step into this portal, into this realm, into this gate, into this place, to trade the goods and services of Heaven into our own lives, which in turn has them trading into other people's lives as they serve them. A greater capacity is drawn from this well—from this place. Understanding this is really taking the load off us where we have had this mindset through religious thinking that we must stir this stuff up inside of us, that we must do these things in and of ourselves.

It is those things coming from this place that allow us to be able to walk in the Fruit of the Spirit and serve others. The pressure has been taken off us. This is the bestowing of these gifts from this place here—this trade route—this glorious trade route. We can step in this realm. We can step in through the gate. This gate was founded at the foundations of creation for people to freely walk, to freely come here, to freely receive. Truth abounds in love. This trading floor is where truth is found abounding in love—love for God's people, love for His sons, and as sons, this is a place that we can come freely.

There are many in the body who feel they fail because they do not truly walk in the Fruit of the Spirit. They cannot pull it out of themselves. They cannot walk in it the way that they want to walk in it. This is how they feel, this is how they perceive themselves. In this place, they can have the understanding that it is not them—it is Him. It is trading *with* Him, because the goods and services of Heaven are for the sons of men. They must step into this place and when they do, they will rejoice in the understanding that it is not in and of themselves, but it is the Father who brings these things out of them, through them, for others. The truest acts of service for others come from this place where love abounds.

How can people think of themselves as failures when it is the Father that is bestowing these things in them and through them through this trade? It will take the pressure off people's hearts and minds that they must muster this in and of themselves. This is Him working through them. This takes the pressure off our soul and our spirit to work anything out because He is doing the work.

We were taken back to the Hall of Commerce and were in awe of the room. It was massive, and it was interesting to me with these small, little offices around the perimeter and how these men and women in white were coming from this trading floor portal. They were going in and out of it, and then going to these offices and getting the trades recorded.

I was reminded of Proverbs 4:7 that reads,

Wisdom is the principal thing; therefore, get wisdom. And in all your getting, get understanding.

That is why Wisdom and Understanding are trades. They trade here with people. When I choose to access wisdom, I choose to accept knowledge, and that is the trade itself.

We immediately found ourselves walking through another door and down a hallway. We passed the Strategy Room and one of the angels waved as we went by. We walked past the Labor and Delivery Room. We went through an entryway into a giant basketball court.

Stephanie asked, "Is this a court (as in judicial) instead of a court (like in a basketball court)? What is this basketball court? I mean, that is what it looks like."

Lydia responded, "There is a place of freedom that people need to really catch hold of things."

Stephanie remarked, "When she said, 'catch hold of,' she threw the ball, and I caught it. There have been a lot of references about balls lately."

Lydia continued, "Freedom is laying down old mindsets and precepts. Freedom is trading, nurturing, walking, and choosing this kingdom principle—that Heaven really is *this* close."

Stephanie said, "Lydia just showed me walking up to a door and kicking the door open."

Lydia explained, "As people gain this knowledge and understanding of the concept of stepping into Heaven—not just stepping into the courts, but being in a place where there is freedom—freedom from the enemy, freedom from old mindsets and precepts, laying it all down—that is what this is.

"We have heard of laying it all down our whole lives. When people choose to realize they can step over the veil—step through the veil—that this access of freedom is for them, it will kick down the walls of old mindsets. We are on the edge of something so profound that people, many people, are going to lay their old mindsets down.

"It is going to kick down the doors and the walls for freedom for people. Keep pressing in. As we do this work, as we say these things, as we tell the people how far the reverberation of this goes, more people are going to be drawn to this because they seek freedom. When they realize that they can trade with Heaven in this way as easily as we have just been shown, the freedom is going to become tangible."

Chapter 14
The Court of Trade

Suddenly, the scene shifted from a basketball court to a courtroom—the Court of Trades. The Court of Trades has a direct link to the Hall of Commerce as if they are together.

Within the court, one could see a large swinging door with men and women in white coming in and out from the Hall of Commerce into the Court of Trade. Men and women in white were bringing paperwork to the Just Judge that was sitting at the Judge's Bench. He was signing papers and stamping them. When the paperwork was complete, the persons in white went back out the door.

The Just Judge turned and looked at us as if to explain that we were about to see how things worked in the Court of Trade. We could see the High Council[24] and see Jesus

---

[24] The High Council consists of men and women in white who judge matters in the earth and in the heavens.

to the left. We were looking at the Judge's Bench and were seated or standing as if in a gallery.

We then saw a person in white coming from the right, bringing paperwork. Someone was standing in front of the Judge with their counsel. The person was seeking a trade of goods and services with the Father.

We could also see what would be either an accuser or a prince, but the accuser was saying that the person could not have full access for the trade because of generational sin and iniquity. Jesus began advocating on behalf of the person, saying that, because of what He did on the cross, that gave the person free access to the trades and goods and services of Heaven.

The Father, the Just Judge, said to the person, "Are you choosing to seek a trade with the goods and services of Heaven?" The person said, "Yes, as an act of my will." Then the Just Judge asked, "Are you choosing to repent on behalf of your generations and to forgive them?"

The person said, "Yes." The accuser began presenting paperwork to the Just Judge who looked at it, while the accuser was saying that the person was indebted with the trading floors of hell.

It seemed as if what we were seeing was in real time, with the Judge going over the paperwork and the accusers off to the side snickering. Jesus was not saying anything, because He already said enough.

The Judge looked at the enemy and said, "He is choosing to trade with Heaven, and I am overturning the trades with hell." Then He handed an eviction notice to the enemy. It said "Eviction Notice" on it.

We then noticed the accuser was wearing a crown and we said, "It's a prince!" This has to do with what we have been learning, regarding striking the parameters, Consequential Liens, and the Trust of Trust with the Father. When we do the work of striking the parameters and getting the Consequential Liens overturned due to this person's act of the will to trade with Heaven with the Father, it is because it is an open Heaven to the sons of men. This also serves as an eviction notice to the prince that is in people's hearts and minds. That is why they started out talking about trading of their hearts and minds.

The prince was served an eviction notice, and he was being taken out in chains. The person was given some paperwork granting them open trade access by trading with Heaven, because of their choice, because they were choosing as an act of their will to trade with the Father; and because this person saw himself as a son. He was then led out of the courtroom. Another person came in and the same thing happened.

What was interesting about this is the people that we saw come in came to the courtroom with the full understanding of themselves—of who they are as a son. As an act of their will, they were saying, "I choose the realms of Heaven." As an act of their will, they said, "I choose the reality. I choose to trade with Heaven."

We understood the reality that they could not do this in and of themselves, and their trading with Heaven was going to give them the Fruit of the Spirit. It was going to give them full access to the goods and services of Heaven, and this was one of the goods right here that we were watching play out—the dismantling of a prince in or upon their generations. That is why it was so important that this was an act of their will.

What was interesting was that the Father kept the legal paperwork from the enemy. He kept it. He did not give it back to the enemy. He gave him an eviction notice instead.

As we watched the court proceedings for the second person, a woman was making a declaration to the Judge that she chooses, as an act of her will, to no longer trade with the trading floors of hell. Rather, as a son, she chooses to trade in the Halls of Commerce with Heaven. Once she made that declaration, we watched as the Father took the paperwork that the enemy had given and He shredded it. He then handed the prince his eviction notice.

The Court Proceedings

The first thing that happens is the person is brought into the court. Jesus is to their left and a man or woman in white comes through the Halls of Commerce and hands the Just Judge the paperwork, which He reads. Jesus says, as an advocate on their behalf, what He has done at the cross. The enemy says that their generations did X, Y, and Z, and they have traded with hell. The Father takes the paperwork and tosses it. When that person says that declaration aloud, then the enemy is handed eviction papers.

That was the process we saw over and over.

We then made a declaration:

We say openly and as an act of our will that we choose to trade with Heaven. We choose to trade with the Halls of Commerce to receive the goods and services from Heaven.

Immediately we found ourselves standing in front of the Judge, and he was handing out an eviction notice.

We looked where Jesus was standing nearby. He was wearing a crown, and He said, "My crown trumps that one every time!"

How do people trade with hell?

Immediately these thoughts came to us:

- Generational iniquities
- Choosing to do wickedness
- Celestial trades that are willful
- Literally making trades

Concerning the work that we are doing with Consequential Liens, this seemed to be the last and final step.

We saw Kevin doing the prayer that we did recently on a Sunday[25] and on a Tuesday[26] when we sent the angels with the capture bags to capture the princes, and then our next step is to seek the eviction notice in the Court of Trades. We step into this court, and as an act of that person's will, they make the statement:

As an act of my will, I choose and I forgive my family for trading with hell, and as an act of my will and on behalf of my family, I choose to trade in the Halls of Commerce.

Once that is done, the Just Judge will issue the eviction notice to the trespassing principalities, and we will be free to trade with Heaven from earth in ways we have never experienced.

---

[25] Referring to a recent gathering of Sandhills Ecclesia which we oversee. Visit SandhillsEcclesia.com.

[26] We conduct an online free mentoring group each Tuesday evening. Register at CourtsOfHeavenWebinars.com.

Chapter 15
Relationships & Trades

As Stephanie and I engaged with Heaven, we had been discussing crossovers[27] relating to the ministry with Ezekiel, our chief ministry angel. Ezekiel explained that crossovers were trying to happen.

We wanted to know, "Is this good? Are these good crossovers?"

He explained, "Crossovers are neutral."

Where there is no agreement, trades do not happen.

Because we had put up a shield around the ministry and we had commissioned Ezekiel, his commanders, and ranks with receiving the things from the Father that are good for the ministry, but keeping out the things that

---

[27] Crossovers are where something or someone outside your life tries to come into your life, or vice versa.

were not. These things will play out differently, depending upon the manner of trade in which the person approaches us.

Understanding Crossovers

This topic is about trade. It is also about building. It's also about navigation and finding the true path. Remember, we can walk with the Spirit of Wisdom. When a person reaches out to us, immediately, we invite the Spirit of Wisdom into the conversation.

The field in which we are sowing has many seeds and yet the harvest of the seeds is still forthcoming. They are growing, but they are not at harvest stage. We have also been amid some crossovers. Some of our leaders are branching out and doing other things within the ministry. These acts are trades through the field of the ministry.

We have many crossovers. At its simplest form, different people in the ministry are doing different things. They are crossing over. Where they have been trading in one form, now they are trading in a new or additional fashion. Within the sphere of the LifeSpring realm we could see what looked like new connections, new bridges—but they were not bridges but links. Different people have been reaching out, and by reaching out, the ministry is expanding. There were those trying to cross into our realm.

We must determine if we will have a trade or not. Remember, we must think in terms of the neutrality of trade. Until an agreement is made, it is neutral. We often think in terms of bad or good, but we know that some things are neutral.

We can give ourselves permission to have a neutrality of thought about someone reaching out to us, and it is just that—it is a neutral place to watch and oversee. Over time, we will obtain direction about what to do about the neutrality in which we hold them—whether to reach out or to retreat.

A trade is made by agreement from both parties. When the agreement feels righteous and when the agreement feels balanced, the trade is made. If not, it can be held in a status of neutrality. The belief system of the heart wants to divide it into positive or negative, but there is a space for neutrality in this situation and holding this neutrality will be needed.

We want an answer from Heaven on what to do about a person. Heaven is telling us, "Hold the person in a neutral place." That is the answer. Sometimes that is not the answer we want or even the answer we thought we were going to get, but it *is* the answer for some situations.

Make space for a space called the place of neutrality. Realize things want to play on the trade. Fear wants to play on the trade. Fear wants to have a say. Fear wants to shape this trade. Other things want to shape the trade. Expectation, memories—these play on the trade. Sometimes we need to hold something in a neutral place.

> *Sometimes we need to hold these things in a neutral place until a moment of time comes where we have a new thought.*

As a watchman, we may have a new thought. We may have a decision. We have our own boundaries. As another thing that can play on a trade, boundaries can play on a trade. These boundaries are God-given—they are the safety net. They provide the safety rails.

In the situation we were thinking of, neither of us felt that a trade was eminent. Because we both felt a boundary line—because of what the person was offering to trade—our boundary lines did not include that trade at this time.

Boundaries are moveable. They are not static in that they can grow with the maturity of the person. They can grow with the calling. They can grow with the realization of a new scroll. They morph. They can change.

> *What we want is the Godhead setting the boundaries for us.*

Not us nor our soul realm changing the boundaries or moving the markers, because the soul realm will do that out of manipulation, out of control, and out of a seeking for power and illegal authority. But we are talking about trade in general.

As we see a trade offer come near, we can hold it in a place of neutrality until we determine where our boundaries are, as given by Father, or what has changed in those boundaries, as related to new scrolls that may or may not have come. Do not forget, our human will is also involved in this, too. We do have choice and the Father honors the human will. It is okay if the human will has decided. The downfall of this occurs when the human will is making the decisions out of the woundedness that is still in one's belief system or out of a heart that is not completely whole. That would be an area to surrender to the Lord so that wholeness comes to that place—so that better willful decisions are made.

For instance, with this person, we felt like we could walk with them in a certain way, but we did not feel easy to walk with them in another way. That was good to notice. Often, some things exist in life where even Heaven is not going to give us the immediate direction, because all things are working together for good. Simply continue to watch, see, and understand. Therefore, walking with Wisdom is needed, and we will begin to gain perspective about it. We could simply say we are in a place of gaining perspective about this. We are going to wait for God's perspective on this.

One of the principles of life is that some people add to our life while others take away. Sometimes, we will have people in our life for a season, and they add to our life. Yet, at the end of that season, allow the relationship to take on the form it needs to take. Do not hold tightly to relationships whose time to end has come. We can part amicably, simply understanding that we both have deposited into the other's life what we were to deposit.

Also, at times our soul longs for a relationship that Heaven knows is not healthy for us to have. We can allow Heaven to build our relationships according to our scrolls. We should not try to build what God does not want to be built in our life. It will only bring misery. Allow Heaven to build our life. Heaven always knows best.

Another way to look at relationships like this, is that in our life some people have refrigerator rights. We have some people in our life that, when they come to our home, we don't mind if they make themselves at home and go to the refrigerator themselves to get something to drink or to get a snack. However, not everyone entering our home has the same level of access to our refrigerator. The internet repairman coming to our home does not have refrigerator rights. However, our best friend who we have known for years does.

Another aspect is not to assume we have rights that we may not have with an individual or ministry. Relationships must be built, and the building of relationships usually takes time. It would be a dishonor to someone to assume refrigerator rights that are not actually bestowed. To assume rights that do not exist may cause a delay in the actual bestowal of those rights. In some cases, these wrong assumptions can cause an abortion of access rights that Heaven may have intended.

Some people have had refrigerator rights with me in the past, but when the relationship is abruptly ended, getting those refrigerator rights restored may not be a quick process. We must choose wisely those in our life who should have refrigerator rights and those who should not. Our life will be simpler and safer for it.

———·———

Chapter 16
Governing Our Realm for Trade

Many humans have not understood their realms, and therefore they have not understood that they have the right to govern their realm. Part of the governing of one's realm is to establish shields of protection. This is the work of angels. Many have seen the need for protection, but few have understood that the shields also work to:

- Allow in the blessings of God
- Allow in the harmony of Heaven
- Allow the love of God
- Allow the associations He wants for us
- Allow the handshakes and the agreements of people that the Father wants us to have so we all can agree.

We have realms, and we are called to govern our realms. All three realms that are in a person's being are to be governed. There are other realms in our realm that intersect. For instance, we intersect the LifeSpring realm, so our realm is working with that realm, and we are helping to govern that realm. We can flow to any of those realms. We want to govern our realms with the help of angels. We can govern them using agreement with God, agreement with what He is doing, agreement with His timeline, agreement with His blessing, and commission our angels to make trades out of our realms—to allow in what the Father is speaking about us and to keep out what He is not speaking about. We can just ask our angels to see to the shields regarding these things.

Here is what strengthens a shield: worship of God; intentional alignment with His Word—spoken and verbalized; the releasing of angels; the request to the Father for angels; the request of things for angels (like elixir and weaponry); and the belief in the angels that He has given to the saints. He has made the angels for co-laboring, and He has given them to us for our good, that we can work with them well and they can do their job. Vocalizing all of this is helpful to these angels who work to keep shields in place.

> *By vocalizing these things aloud, we help establish them in the atmosphere about us.*

When talking of governing ourselves, we are talking about a person, a three-part person: spirit, soul, and body. If we are talking about the spirit of that person, that spirit has a realm. That person's spirit must govern their realm. They can govern their realm with spiritual truth, with spiritual belief, with spiritual faith, with spiritual sight, and with spiritual activity. Remember that realms intersect and overlap. The realms both intersect from the innermost part (our spirit to our soul) and both also to our body realm (the container for the spirit and soul).

Our realm trades with other realms. The intent of our realm is to trade with other realms that have righteous trades to trade with us, so we can trade with them.

Take for example, Tom.[28] Tom had a trade with us that we are aware of. He was trying to expand the trade, but we were not in agreement with the trade that he was wanting to expand. We had a problem with it, so what was happening was his trading with us had been misaligned. He had a previous trade with us, but when he made it, the new trade was outside of the previous trade he had made. We were not willing to make the new trade, and because we were not willing to make that trade, the intersection of the realms could not happen.

What was happening was we were putting up or we were enforcing our shield against the trade, but the transaction could not have a resolution until we had heard back from his sphere in his realm. We believed that it was an unrighteous trade that he was trying to make—not because it was bad, but because it was outside of the boundaries of the original trade. Therefore, we were not receiving the new trade into our realm. The

---

[28] A fictional name.

agreement did not feel balanced to us. One was being asked to give more than one was willing to give. That is a definition of being stolen from. The frustration from that situation creates a dissonance between the realms.

What exacerbates this dissonance is the lack of communication regarding what we are willing to trade and not willing to trade. When we communicate to Tom where we stand—what we are not willing to trade, then his realm will either align or retreat. If the choice is retreat, that's not negative. Do not put that in a good or bad category. It is a neutral category. Retreat means he is gone—he is retreating to think about it. He will either agree or he will retreat. If he retreats, he may come back with another thing, or he may just take time to agree.

How shall two walk together, lest they agree? [29]

The Shields[30]

We want to commission our angels to work with what is meant to come through, because some things are meant to come through our shield. How will we know what is meant to come through our shield? They will have been written into books of Heaven about us.

Commission our angels to allow into our realm the things that are written in Heaven about us: the words of

---

[29] Amos 3:3
[30] For more about shields, see my book *Commissioning Angels*, LifeSpring Publishing (2022)

the Father, the books written about us in Heaven, the maps about us in Heaven, the potentials about us in Heaven. We want these things in *the measured flow* of Heaven to our realms. We have a role in this to work with the angels—to accommodate the trades, even with Heaven, with people, with structures, etc.

Declaration & Commission for Erecting Shields & Governing Realms[31]

I call the angels assigned to me to come near.

[Await the sense of their arrival. Once we sense their arrival], verbally say:

I am a realm. I choose to govern my spirit realm in the name of Jesus through the love of God for me through my salvation—through my redemption in Christ Jesus, I govern my realm by agreement with God, agreement with what He is doing, agreement with His timeline, agreement with His blessing, and I commission my angels to make trades out of my realms to allow in what the Father is speaking about me, and to keep out what He is not speaking about me.

---

[31] More teaching about engaging and co-laboring with angels and angelic commissions can be found in the books *Commissioning Angels* and *Engaging Angels in the Realms of Heaven* by Dr. Ron Horner.

I commission my angels to see to the shields regarding these things. I choose to govern my realms with the help of angels, by agreement with God: agreement with what He is doing, agreement with His timeline, and agreement with His blessing.

I also choose to govern my soul realm, that it may grow and learn via my spirit the things of Heaven, so that my mind is renewed in the ways of the Kingdom of God. I choose to feed my spirit only that which is beneficial. I also choose to govern my body realm, that it be a healthy carrier of my spirit and soul realms, and that I be able to glorify God in my body.

I commission my spirit to govern my realm with spiritual truth, spiritual belief, spiritual faith, spiritual sight, and with spiritual activity.

I commission my angels to allow into my realm the things that are written in Heaven about me; the words of the Father, the books written about me in Heaven, the maps and keys for me in Heaven, the potentials about me in Heaven.

I want these things in the measured flow of Heaven to my realms.

I choose to work with the angels to accommodate the trades Heaven desires—with Heaven, people, and structures.

I commission my personal angels to erect my personal shields.

I commission my angels to engage the shields that are to be erected by Heaven for my life.

I commission my angels to work with Ezekiel, his commanders, and ranks regarding the shields they have erected and to work with the shield function of LifeSpring International Ministries.

I commission my angels to work with what is meant to come through these shields according to my book and to use and help me use my maps and keys.

I commission my angels to make trades out of my realms to allow in what the Father is speaking about me and to keep out what He is not speaking about.

I commission my angels to see to the shields regarding these things.

I commission my angels to work with the angels assigned to LifeSpring International Ministries to develop the shield all around my spirit realm, to strengthen it, to support it, to engage it, to keep it activated, and to see to it.

I commission my angels to allow in the blessings of God, the harmony of Heaven, the love of God, the associations He wants for me, the handshakes, and the agreements of people that the Father wants for me so we can all agree with the purposes and desire of God.

I also commission my angels to help me understand where a breach has happened in a shield so that I can work together with the angels to strengthen the shield.

I choose to strengthen my shield by the worship of God; by intentional alignment with His Word— spoken and verbalized; by the releasing of angels; by request of the Father for angels, by the request of things for angels (like elixir and weaponry); and by my belief in them, and that He has given them and made them for co-laboring; and He has given them to me for my good. I choose to work with them, so they do their job.

I declare these things in the name of Jesus Christ and commission the angels assigned to me to these things in time and out of time, in Jesus' name.

———·———

Chapter 17
Conclusion

When I first was approached by Heaven about understanding trade and the celestial realm, it was far outside my comfortable box. However, I have been willing to have my box reconstructed, if not demolished altogether. As these changes have occurred in my mindset, many old ways of thinking have had to go. I have had to evaluate and eliminate every vestige of a poverty mindset. How do we know that is an issue? Notice how we use our tube of toothpaste. Do we attempt to squeeze every drop of paste out of the tube? Do we keep the Cool Whip® container or the butter tub so we can reuse it later? Do our cabinets look like a plastic recycling center?

We often act as if we will never be able to go to the grocery store again or the local department store. We act as if they won't make any more bowls that are designed for reuse.

Adina and I visited an elderly lady we knew once, and upon entering her kitchen, we saw empty one-gallon milk jugs stacked to the ceiling along with washed 2-liter soda bottles, also stacked to the ceiling. Cool Whip containers and margarine tubs were stacked as well. She would never in her lifetime use all the containers she was saving for that "rainy day." Unfortunately, she had a poverty mindset. She loved God but felt it necessary to save every container that might be used by someone someday.

Another clue to a poverty mindset is seen when we listen to someone speak on Christian stewardship, tithing, and giving offerings, and we kick back on what we are hearing. We are resisting, and often the resistance is fear-based. Heaven is trying to teach us the lesson Jesus was teaching His disciples with the feeding of the 5,000 and later the feeding of the 4,000. The lesson was simple: where Jesus is, we have enough. We never have lack when Jesus is in the room.

Jesus knew how to trade with Heaven. He knew how to access the resources of Heaven, even to the point of a fish swallowing a coin so that He and Peter could pay their taxes. Trading with Heaven is simply learning to exchange what is in our hand for what is in our Father's hand, and His hand is immensely large. Let's not be stingy. Let's make the trade!

Appendix

Learning to Live Spirit First

A challenge with how we were taught about the Christian life is that everything was put off until sometime in the future. Then, we read the letters of Paul, and we experienced a disconnect. Heaven, to us, was a destination, not a resource. We knew nothing about learning to live from our spirits. We only knew what we had been doing all our lives, and that is to live to satisfy our soul or our flesh. We sorely need to learn an alternative way of living.

Exchanging Our Way of Living

Paul recorded these words in his letter to the Romans:

Those who are motivated by the flesh only pursue what benefits themselves. But those who live by

> *the impulses of the Holy Spirit are motivated to pursue spiritual realities. (Romans 8:5) (TPT)*

We must learn to live spirit first! We must exchange our way of living. We must learn to live from our spirit. We need to understand the hierarchy within us:

- We are a spirit.
- We possess a soul.
- We live in body.

Each component has a specific purpose in our lives. Our spirit is the interface with the supernatural realm. It is designed for interfacing with Heaven and the Kingdom realm. Our spirit has been in existence in our body since our conception. Our soul has a different purpose. It communicates to our intellect and our physical body what our spirit has obtained from Heaven. It is the interface with our body. Our body houses the two components and will follow the dictates of whichever component is dominating,

Most of us have never been taught about having our spirit dominate. Rather, we have merely assumed that our soul being dominant was the required mode of operation.

Our soul always wants to be in charge. Our soul is susceptible to carnal or fleshly desires, lusts, and behaviors. It will, at times, resist our spirit and body. It must be made to submit to our spirit by an act of our will.

Our will is a means of instructing either component (spirit, soul, or body) what to do. Our soul has a will, and so does our spirit. We choose who dominates!

Our body, on the other hand, has appetites that will control us in subjection to our soul. Do they become partners in crime? Remember that second piece of chocolate cake it wanted? Our body will try, along with our soul, to dictate our behavior. It will resist the spirit's domination of our life. However, it will obey our spirit's domination if instructed, and our body can aid our spirit if trained to do so.

The typical expression that operates in most people's lives is that their soul is first, body second, and their spirit is somewhere in the distance, in last place.

In some people, especially those very conscious of their physical fitness or physical appearance, there is a different lineup. Their body is their priority, the soul second, and again their spirit is the lowest priority.

Heaven's desire for us is vastly different. Heaven desires that we live spirit first, soul second, and body third. Since we are spiritual beings, this is the optimal arrangement. For most of us, our spirit was not activated in our life in any measure until we became born again.

If, after our salvation experience, we began to pursue our relationship with the Father, then we became much more aware of our spirit and learning to live more spirit conscious. The apostle Paul wrote in his various epistles about living in the spirit or walking in the spirit. Because we are spiritual beings, our spirits cry out for a deepening of relationship with the Father. Our spirit longs for it and will try to steer us in that direction.

Our soul has certain characteristics that explain its behavior in our life. This is the briefest of lists, but I think we will get the idea. Our soul is selfish. It wants what it wants when it wants it. It can be very pouty. It can act like a small child. It is offendable and often even looks for opportunities to be offended. Our soul is also rude.

Our body has a distinct set of characteristics. It is inconsiderate, demanding, lazy, and self-serving. It does not want to get out of bed in the morning, for many people. In others, it wants to be fed things that are not beneficial.

However, characteristics of our spirit are hugely different. If we live out of our spirit, we will find that we are loving and prone to be gentle. We desire peace. We are considerate. We are far more contented when living out of our spirit. Also, joy will often have great expression in our lives.

Sometimes, we have experienced traumas that create a situation of our soul not trusting our spirit. The soul blames the spirit for not protecting it. The irony is that typically, our soul never gave place to the spirit so that it could protect us. The soul places false blame on the spirit, and it must be coerced to forgive the spirit. Then the soul must relinquish control to the spirit. Once the soul forgives the spirit, the two components can begin to work in harmony.

If I were to flash an image of some delicious, freshly cooked donuts in front of us, what would happen? For many, their body would announce a craving for one. What if, instead, I showed an image of a bowl of broccoli? How many people would get excited about that? Not as much excitement over a bowl of broccoli would be exhibited. Which does our body prefer—the donuts or the broccoli? For the untamed soul, the donuts are likely to win out every time. Which do most kids prefer?

In any case, we can train ourselves to go for the healthier option. A principle regarding this that I heard years ago is summed up like this:

What we feed will live—
what we starve will die

What do we want to be dominant—our spirit, our soul, or our body? The part we feed is the part that will dominate.

For some, they feed their soul and live by the logic of their mind. Everything must be reasoned out in their mind before they will accept it. However, because our soul gains its insight from the Tree of the Knowledge of Good and Evil, it will always have faulty and limited understandings.

How do we change this soul-dominant or body-dominant pattern? We instruct our soul to back up, and we call our spirit to come forward. Some people may need to physically stand up, and speak to their soul and say, "Soul, back up." As they say those words, they can take a physical step backward. Then, they can speak to their spirit aloud and say, "Spirit, come forward." As we speak those words, take a physical step forward. This prophetic act helps trigger a shift within them.

Live spirit first!

Benefits of Living Spirit First

Why would we want to live spirit first? Let me present several reasons. Living spirit first will create in us an increased awareness of Heaven and the realms of Heaven. It will create a deeper comprehension of the presence of Holy Spirit, of angels, and men and women in white linen. We will be able to better hear the voice of Heaven. We will experience greater creativity, productivity, hope, and peace. We will become more aware of the needs of people that we can meet.

As we live spirit first, we will be able to access the riches of Heaven in our life. Petty things that formerly bothered us will dissipate in importance or impact in our life. We will be able to move ahead, not concerning ourselves with the petty, mundane, or unproductive things that have affected our life before we began to live spirit first.

This way of life is more than a game changer—for the believer, it is the only way to live. We will face challenges as we build our business or live our life from Heaven down™, but we will more readily be able to access the solutions of Heaven as we live with an awareness of the richness of Heaven and all that is available to us as a son or daughter of the Lord Most High. Do not live dominated by the soul. *Live spirit first!*

——— · ———

Description

What we refer to as commerce, Heaven refers to as trade. It is the exchange of something of value from one party to another. We practice trades every day. Someone may choose to take a moment to trade time for information to determine if this book will be of benefit. Should a person decide that it would be beneficial, then they will make a trade of currency for the product.

The process of heavenly trade has been occurring since before Adam and Eve. If we as sons learn the principles and processes of trade, we will be able to engage Heaven on a deeper level and be able to impact our communities on a greater scale.

We need to understand that worship is trade, gaining knowledge is trade, prayer is trade, and pouring out one's life for another is trade. The universe revolves around, but the sons must ensure that trade is done in a Godly manner. Learn some principles of trade, and learn to live our life in a new light.

About the Author

Dr. Ron Horner is a communicator and author of several bestsellers. He writes and teaches on the Courts of Heaven, as well as how to engage Heaven, and how to live from Heaven down™, having written over twenty books. His work has taken him around the globe. Ron is the founder of LifeSpring International Ministries, which serves to advocate for individuals and businesses in the Courts of Heaven.

Ron teaches a weekly Mentoring Group on the Courts of Heaven primarily and conducts seminars regularly. He is also founder of Heaven down™ Business, a worldwide consulting firm (HeavenDownBusiness.com).

———·———

Other Books by Dr. Ron M. Horner

Building Your Business from Heaven Down

Building Your Business from Heaven Down 2.0

Commissioning Angels – Volume 1

Cooperating with The Glory

Courts of Heaven Process Charts

Dealing with Trusts, & Consequential Liens

Engaging Angels in the Realms of Heaven

Engaging Heaven for Revelation – Volume 1

Engaging Heaven for Revelation – Volume 2

Engaging the Courts for Ownership & Order

Engaging the Courts for Your City (Paperback, Leader's Guide & Workbook)

Engaging the Courts of Healing & the Healing Garden

Engaging the Courts of Heaven

Engaging the Help Desk of the Courts of Heaven

Engaging the Mercy Court of Heaven

Four Keys to Dismantling Accusations

Freedom from Mithraism

Kingdom Dynamics – Volume 1

Let's Get it Right!

Lingering Human Spirits

Lingering Human Spirits – Volume 2

Living Spirit Forward

Overcoming the False Verdicts of Freemasonry

Overcoming Verdicts from the Courts of Hell

Releasing Bonds from the Courts of Heaven

Unlocking Spiritual Seeing

SPANISH

Cómo Proceder en la Corte Celestial de Misericordia

Las Cuatro Llaves para Anular las Acusaciones

Liberando Bonos en las Cortes Celestiales

Liberando Su Visión Espiritual

Sea Libre del Mitraísmo

Tablas de Proceso de la Cortes del Cielo

Viviendo desde el Espíritu

———— · ————

www.ingramcontent.com/pod-product-compliance
Lightning Source LLC
Chambersburg PA
CBHW031631160426
43196CB00006B/361